T0150714

FIGHT
TO WIN

MARTIN J. DOUGHERTY

FIGHT TO WIN

20 SIMPLE TECHNIQUES THAT WILL WIN ANY FIGHT

TUTTLE Publishing

Tokyo | Rutland, Vermont | Singapore

Published by Tuttle Publishing, an imprint of Periplus Editions (HK) Ltd.

www.tuttlepublishing.com

Library of Congress Cataloging-in-Publication Data In Process

ISBN: 978-0-8048-4268-6

Distributed by

North America, Latin America & Europe
Tuttle Publishing
364 Innovation Drive
North Clarendon, VT 05759-9436 U.S.A.
Tel: 1 (802) 773-8930
Fax: 1 (802) 773-6993
info@tuttlepublishing.com
www.tuttlepublishing.com

Japan
Tuttle Publishing
Yaekari Building,
3rd Floor, 5-4-12 Osaki
Shinagawa-ku
Tokyo 141 0032
Tel: (81) 3 5437-0171
Fax: (81) 3 5437-0755
sales@tuttle.co.jp
www.tuttle.co.jp

Asia Pacific
Berkeley Books Pte. Ltd.
61 Tai Seng Avenue
#02-12, Singapore 534167
Tel: (65) 6280-1330
Fax: (65) 6280-6290
inquiries@periplus.com.sg
www.periplus.com

First edition
16 15 14 13   5 4 3 2 1   1307CP

Printed in Singapore

TUTTLE PUBLISHING® is a registered trademark of Tuttle Publishing, a division of Periplus Editions (HK) Ltd.

Contents

Disclaimer

Please note that the publisher and author(s) of this instructional book are NOT RESPONSIBLE in any manner whatsoever for any injury that may result from practicing the techniques and/or following the instructions given within. Martial arts training can be dangerous—both to you and to others—if not practiced safely. If you're in doubt as to how to proceed or whether your practice is safe, consult with a trained martial arts teacher before beginning. Since the physical activities described herein may be too strenuous in nature for some readers, it is also essential that a physician be consulted prior to training.

Acknowledgments

Thanks are due to many people who assisted in various ways: Rick Burns and the members of Burns School of Black Belts for their assistance and the use of their venue.

Chris Wilson and the members of SDF Peterlee, for their assistance.

The many people who have taught me, but most notably Dave Turton.

Gavin Lanata and Paul Green for being accommodating about camera stuff.

Nate Zettle for so many things that it'd take the rest of the book to catalog them.

Introduction

This book is about winning fights. It presents a simple, easy-to-learn body of technique along with the psychological, tactical, and technical factors needed to make it work. The techniques presented here are equally applicable to self-defense and sporting applications, though not all of them are legal in every type of competition.

The techniques in this book are found, in some shape or form, in most martial arts and at least some are likely to be familiar to any given martial artist. This does not mean that the techniques in this book are the best possible versions of the most effective techniques for any given situation. Instead, they were chosen for their ease of use and flexibility. They will get the job done under almost any circumstances, without needing a lengthy period of training to achieve effectiveness.

The system presented here is—as the title of the book suggests—a shortcut to combat effectiveness. If you can do everything presented here, do it well and do it at the right time, then you will be an extremely effective fighter. Reaching that level of skill and ability will not take very long, because the techniques are simple and there is a fairly small number of them. The intent is to reach a solid level of all-round capability as quickly as possible. From this base, it is possible to progress in several directions, but as a general rule it is better to become very skilled with a small number of techniques than to collect dozens of variations.

While this book does allow a fighter to take a shortcut through the maze of available techniques, there is still no substitute for hard training—ideally with a good instructor or at least a competent partner. The shortcut is in terms of content, that is, not having to waste time learning a vast body of graded technique before getting to what you need, or going down blind alleys while experimenting with techniques. It is still necessary to put in the time to become skilled at these techniques and the system that binds them together. However, the time required to become highly skilled with twenty techniques is obviously going to be less than that required for several dozen.

Whether competition or "street," a fight is an unpleasant environment to be in, where nothing ever goes according to plan. Simple techniques done well are a better option than flashy or overcomplex moves, despite how good they look in training.

With an attack coming in, it is necessary to do something about it right now, rather than the perfect thing a second too late. If what you do works well enough to keep you in the fight, then that's good enough.

There is no intent here to insult any martial art, nor to suggest that much of a given system is useless. The body of technique in any martial art exists for a reason, and there is much to learn from a full and formal art. However, the purpose of most martial arts classes is not to produce an effective all-round fighter in the shortest possible time. This book is aimed at those whose goal is to become such a fighter, whether or not they also train in a formal martial art.

Most of the techniques in this book are equally applicable to Mixed Martial Arts (MMA) and self-defense. Some are more appropriate in a sporting context; some are illegal in most forms of competition. Applications are discussed when each technique is presented. All the techniques are found in mainstream martial arts, though not all of them will be contained within any given art. Thus, a judo player will be familiar with the takedowns and chokes, though he may give them different names, and a kickboxer will find that most of the strikes are contained in his art. These techniques are found at the core of fighting systems that have been in use for centuries, for the very good reason that they work.

There are various names for the techniques covered here. We will use generic titles for simplicity, highlighting similar techniques in common martial arts. As a rule, a technique that does the same job in roughly the

Often there are underlying principles that make techniques work. The concept of "broken balance" is vital to many restraints, standing submissions, and takedowns. On the right, balance is broken by bending him backwards, making it very difficult to resist or counter the hold.

same way can be considered to be equivalent. If your "home" art has a workable technique that fills the same niche as one presented here,"then you would be well advised to use the one you already know rather than trying to learn another way to get the same job done. After all, if you already have a chrome spanner, why go out and buy one that's been painted yellow? It's the same tool and it does the same job.

Remember, our aim here is to develop combat effectiveness, not to learn a specific group of techniques and impress a panel of grading judges with them. That is the underlying theme throughout the book —no matter how scrappy or messy a technique looks, if it works then it's a good one. Techniques are tools for winning fights. They need to be performed well to get good results, but it is the result that matters. Sloppy technique can be fixed later; a lost fight will stay lost.

Your "combat toolkit" must be flexible enough to be applied in many different situations. In most cases there's no rocket science involved— a punch is pretty much a punch whether it's delivered standing up or in ground-and-pound. The hard part is putting yourself where that punch can be most effectively delivered.

CHAPTER 1

Martial Artist or Fighter?

Martial Arts and Personal Combat

The term "martial art" can be defined as "fighting system," or perhaps "military (or warrior) skills." All martial arts have their origins in personal combat, often in a military context. However, over time the focus has drifted, and today the various activities that come under the heading of martial arts are quite varied. Not all martial arts have fighting as their focus, and some really have nothing to do with combat any more.

Some arts are geared more towards fitness, sport, personal development, the preservation of traditional systems, and all kinds of other goals. This does not make any of them intrinsically good or bad. If an art does what it is supposed to—like looking amazing on demonstrations, or instilling confidence and self-discipline in children—and does it well, then it is by definition good for its stated purpose and a worthy endeavor in its own right.

For our purposes, though, we are mostly interested in combat effectiveness and it is fair to say that some arts are more useful for personal combat

The axe kick looks awesome but it's very hard to land one in a serious fight. The time spent learning to perform such difficult techniques is better spent on bread-and-butter skills.

than others. However, even the best fighting system has weak areas and blind spots. Finding them and plugging the gaps is the primary reason for a system to evolve over time. Early Mixed Martial Arts competitions demonstrated the need to be an all-around fighter. A combatant who can exploit the gaps in his opponent's capabilities can win an easy victory, so it is logical to develop the capability to deal with all of the likely threats. Equally, some capabilities are not necessary to some martial arts due to their competition rules.

It is important to view any given martial art in this light. For example, a striking art that does not allow any form of grappling or punches to the head in its competitions has obvious weak areas when outside these artificial constraints. It is optimized for a particular style of combat and is strong there. For example, ju-jitsu and judo contain many of the same throws and takedowns, but a ju-jitsu practitioner is expected to also learn striking and many submissions that are not contained in the judo body of technique. Which is better? That depends entirely on what you want to do with it. If your aim is to do well in judo competition, then you would be well advised to train in judo. For more general applications, ju-jitsu is more flexible.

A given martial art is not "bad" or "useless" if it does not cover one or another aspect of personal combat, but it may not be a good choice if all-round capability is your goal. Many highly focused arts contain excellent techniques within their own arena but are weak elsewhere. The only time this is a problem is when an instructor of one of those arts discounts a threat his students are ill-equipped to deal with effectively.

There is little point in training to fight from the clinch in a sport where the fighters are quickly separated, such as boxing. Clinch work is vital for more general applications, not least as a transition stage between "standup" and your "ground game."

So it is perfectly fine to say something like, "we're teaching non-contact karate. It's excellent for fitness, self-discipline and we clean up in non-contact point fighting competitions" if that's true. The same instructor claiming "We're teaching non-contact karate, the ultimate fighting system ever. Grapplers? Pah, you just kick them right off the planet before they can grab you!" may actually not realize that what he is saying is untrue, but nevertheless it is a misleading claim.

It is necessary to be realistic about martial arts when seeking somewhere to train. A "good" art does what it is supposed to, whatever that may be. Good does not always equate to ideal for personal combat though. It is worth looking at a few different classes before committing to something. However, just because an art is not the ultimate all-round fighting system does not mean you should pass it up. If you enjoy it and get something out of it, then it's a good place to train. There is nothing to stop you going to a class for fun and working on fight-winning skills elsewhere.

Self-defense vs. Sport

The "Street vs. Sport" debate has probably raged for as long as there have been streets and combat sports. The crux of the argument is that the sporting environment is different to that encountered outside a pizza shop at 2 a.m., and the real or imagined differences between the two are used as ammunition by those who claim that various martial arts techniques will or will not work "on the street."

The truth is that there are indeed differences between a sporting environment and "real" personal combat. There are also a number of close similarities. Assuming that you are not expecting to wrestle crocodiles or

"Sport" groundfighting is subject to artificial rules about what you can and can't do. The fighter who makes best use of position and leverage will be able to apply a submission technique and win....

... which really isn't any different to "Street" groundfighting. You just have a few more tools at your disposal and some nasty dirty tricks to watch out for. Position and leverage are still the keys to success, whatever sort of ground you're fighting on.

something, your likely opponent will be built like most other human beings. Maybe a bit bigger or smaller, but in possession of the same number of arms, legs, and heads, equipped with the same weapons and vulnerable in the same places.

The fact that humans are all put together in much the same way means that they tend to do much the same things in a fight. There are cultural and environmental differences of course, but as a rule the instincts to grab and strike are the same the world over. Thus the things that work in a cage match are surprisingly similar to those that work when rolling around in the street outside a nightclub.

Generally speaking, the victor in a fight will be the fighter who:
• Makes best use of his own physical capabilities
• Prevents the opponent from utilizing his own advantages
• Takes into account any environmental factors

The first two are self-explanatory—fight better than the other guy and don't let him do what he wants to if you can avoid it. The third is a little more subtle. Environmental factors can include things like showing the judges what they need to see in order to award you victory, making use of the limited space in a ring or fighting area as well as various "street" factors.

Dojo, cage, ring, or street; the same basic principles apply to effective fighting. If you can break the opponent's posture and/or control his head, his options are severely limited.

Any grappling situation will be chracterized by move and counter-move, with the position of the fighters dictating what options are available. Pulling the head down will get someone under control, the response is grabbing the leg and trying to overbalance the opponent.

These include the presence of your friends, the opponent's friends and any bystanders who might become involved plus traffic, curbs, broken glass, and anything else that might influence the course of a fight.

The primary difference between "street" and "sport" are that in a sporting event there are rules, (usually) weight categories and other factors intended to create a reasonably fair fight, and relatively minor consequences in the case of defeat. An opponent who throws in the towel or taps out in a sporting event is likely to be safe, and on the opposite side of that coin, an opponent who gives up is no longer a threat. He is not likely to start throwing punches as soon as you let go of him.

Conversely, there is no guarantee that a "street" opponent will not beg for mercy then attack you after you have released him. His friends or random passers-by may decide to join in, or there may be weapons involved. You cannot guarantee good footing and a suitable fight environment. There is also likely to be some doubt and confusion about whether or not a fight is about to start, whereas in a sporting event you will know what you are expected to do, and when.

However, fighting skills are fighting skills. It has been suggested that a "street" opponent can bite and gouge eyes, making conventional grappling skills invalid. The first half of that sentence is true; the second does not necessarily follow. After all, biting and eye-gouging are just tools, just like an armbar or a choke. Fighting skills are about using the tools you have at your disposal and stopping the opponent from using his. Whether the tool is an armlock or a bite, the positional skills you learn in training will help you use your tools and defend against those of the opponent.

It is necessary to tailor your tactics to the situation. Striking is not allowed in a judo match so you can expect your opponent not to punch you in the face. Instead, you must watch for attempts to throw you or take you down. In a street fight, with a risk that someone might run up and kick you while you work your opponent, trying to set up an armbar on the ground might not be an ideal tactic. You can usually afford to take your time in a sporting match, which may not be an option under "street" circumstances.

One of the key fighting skills that you need to develop is to appraise the situation and adapt to it. The skills you use are much the same; for example you can use groundfighting skills to disengage from a "street" attacker who has managed to take you down, or to obtain a submission from a sporting opponent. The skills are much the same; the important thing is to use them intelligently and to adapt to the situation.

Habits can be dangerous in this context. If you routinely train in an environment with rules against striking or grappling, it is possible to become over-fixated with one mode of combat, and to develop a blind spot regard-

Very few techniques have only one application. The "arm wrap" movement normally used to trap an arm can also give you control of an opponent's leg, which can protect from being kicked.

ing possible attacks. This can be overcome by occasionally changing the rules during application work such as rolling, sparring, or self-defense drills.

There is nothing complex about any of this; it is simply a matter of being realistic about what will work in a given environment and fighting accordingly. The basic principles of personal combat are exactly the same for the street as they are for the sporting environment. The ability to adapt to changing circumstances is one of the hallmarks of an effective fighter. A good fighter is a good fighter wherever they happen to be.

Winning A Fight

Winning simply means making the fight end on the most favorable terms you can obtain. Sometimes it is possible to emerge victorious and unscathed; on other occasions the price of victory can be high. As a rule, more effective fighters take less punishment on the way to victory, but there is more to this than simple fighting ability. The best way to avoid getting hurt in a fight is to make it end quickly, which requires a combination of techniques, tactics, and psychological factors.

There are three ways a fight can end: self-stop, inability to continue, or intervention. Multiple variations of each exist, but all fall under these general headings.

Self-stop

Self-stop occurs when one combatant decides not to fight any more. This can take the form of surrender, voluntary collapse or a choice to break off. In a sporting context, the most common form of surrender is tapping out.

Some submissions do not cause harm but hurt so much that most opponents will tap out if they cannot escape. Opponents with a huge pain tol-

On the left, the arm is isolated and all he has to do is crank the lock. Resisting will just result in injury, so tapping out will indicate concession of the bout. This is the most common form of self-stop in a sporting contest.

erance, or who are drunk or drugged, may not submit despite incredible pain. The threat of physical damage, or the ability to inflict damage, may be necessary to get some opponents to submit. Pain alone, or just holding someone in place, is rarely enough to make the opponent give up. The combination of pain and helplessness, i.e. a situation where only submission will make the pain stop, is far more effective than just one or the other.

It is possible to take the fight out of some assailants by applying a painful restraint or submission, and warning them of what will happen if they carry on fighting. This is only worth trying if you think there is a reasonable chance of success. Someone who is clearly determined to fight will not self-stop in this manner.

Self-stop can occur before actual violence begins, for example where a potential assailant realizes that you could hurt him quite badly and decides that finding an easier target might be a good idea. The same can happen during a fight when one opponent realizes that he is getting the worst of it, or that the price of victory will be higher than he is prepared to pay. Sometimes an opponent panics and begins to desperately try to get away, but more often self-stop occurs when, for whatever reason, the combatants move apart and there is an instant to take stock of the situation.

It is important to be able to recognize an opponent who has self-stopped. The condition does not always last; sometimes an opponent will get back into a fighting mindset. It is critical to exploit the situation while it lasts. In a sporting context, an opponent who has given up in his mind but has not conceded the bout presents an opportunity to finalize the victory. A determined attack at this point may cause him to simply fold up, or the referee may end the bout. Even if this is not the case, you can still press your advantage while the opponent is mentally out of the fight. By the time he pulls himself together you will have tipped the odds even further in your favor.

In a self-defense situation, an opponent who has self-stopped will often posture and make threats—usually while walking backwards away from you—to save face. At this point you have won providing you do not give him a reason to get back into the fight. He will most likely retreat behind a barrage of abuse and threats. If you let him go, the matter is over. If, on the other hand, you show weakness (e.g. by dropping your guard) or say something that pricks his ego and makes him angry enough to come back for another go, then you will have to fight him all over again.

An opponent who is moving away from you is almost certainly not inclined to fight, but someone who says the same words while staying close to you is still a threat. Correctly reading the situation will allow you to bring the matter to a close without further effort. The opponent will probably go and tell other people that he won, or that he would have if only… whatever reason he invents… had happened. That does not really matter; what is important is that you have ended the situation on reasonably favorable terms. Your ego might like it better if you battered the opponent senseless, but it is not necessary. And of course, whatever the opponent might say, you both know what really happened. He gave up; you won.

Self-stop can also take the form of voluntary collapse. This occurs when one fighter cannot take any more and goes down. Exhaustion often causes a fighter to give up—a blow that would have been merely painful in the first round may cause a boxer to fold up and go down in round nine, simply because his will to continue has been eroded by weariness. The decision to give up is not always conscious; it is often triggered by self-preservation instincts.

A fighter who is down and winded may be physically capable of getting back to his feet and carrying on, though most likely in a feeble manner that will merely invite more damage. He has an opportunity for voluntary collapse, and it may well be the right decision. Fighting on until you are too broken to even get up may be admirable in some ways, but it achieves little and is unlikely to result in a victory. Going down, or staying down for the count, might be the right decision. It might also be the only possible option—the will to fight can be broken just as the body can be damaged.

This is especially true in a sporting contest, where survival is not threatened. Sometimes a fighter subconsciously decides that he is taking too much damage for what is at stake. A knockdown or a momentary pause provides an opportunity to collapse, ending the bout. This subconscious decision to give up can be overridden by a determined fighter, but only so many times. Everyone has their limits.

A fighter who is down but not out has a tough decision to make: get up and risk taking more punishment, or accept defeat? Fatigue and pain can wear down a fighter until he just can't go on.

It is easy to be contemptuous of someone who chooses to go down to a blow that they could have taken and fought on, or who taps out to a painful but not damaging submission. However, it is not as simple as that. A fight is more than an exchange of physical techniques; combatants attack one other's will to fight at the same time as they inflict pain and damage on the body and attempt to tire one another out.

These three factors—physical damage, tiredness, and the erosion of the will to fight—are all interrelated. A fighter who gives up easily may be worthy of contempt perhaps, but one who is worn down in a tough contest deserves respect whether his inability to fight on stems from exhaustion, damage, or mental defeat.

Inability to Continue

Inability can occur for two reasons; either the opponent is physically unable to continue fighting, or he is prevented from doing so by some means. The latter could be because you have escaped. If you can run away, get to the other side of a door and lock it, or put some other barrier in the way then the fight cannot continue. This is not really applicable to a sporting bout, unless you want to jump out of the ring and leg it into the changing rooms. It is, however, a valid gambit in a self-defense situation.

It is even possible to consider escape as a "win." If you were sufficiently overmatched that you would suffer serious injury then an escape, however undignified, is a better outcome. However, the "just run away" school of self-defense thinking is rather limited. There is no point in fleeing from someone who is likely to pursue and catch you; you'll just have to fight when you're tired. Escape is a tool for ending a fight like any other but it must be used intelligently.

If it is not possible to escape and the opponent cannot be induced to give up (i.e. self-stop), then the only option is to render him physically incapable of fighting. There are two ways to do this; either by inflicting sufficient harm on his body that he cannot use it to fight with, or by switching off the control mechanism by inducing unconsciousness. That can be achieved by blows to the head, by causing the head to strike something, or by the use of a choke or strangle. The latter is safe enough if you know what you are doing, but can cause death if kept on too long.

The simplest way of inducing an inability to continue, in principle at least, is a knockout blow to the head. However, in practice, this can be hard to deliver; mainly because the opponent will protect his head. Temporary inability can be induced by winding the opponent with a body blow, which might also lead to a self-stop. Alternatively, it is possible to damage body parts so that they cannot be used.

Most of the techniques normally termed joint locks and submissions were originally designed to destroy or disable a joint. In a sporting context they are usually applied firmly and steadily, causing pain and the threat of injury if the opponent does not submit. Continued pressure will cause damage to the joint, or alternatively the lock can be slammed on hard and fast with no attempt at control. This gives the opponent no chance to tap out and would only be done in self-defense, where the intent is to disable an assailant rather than to win a sporting contest.

Intervention

Intervention in a sporting context can take the form one fighter's corner "throwing in the towel," sometimes literally. This is one responsibility of the corner man—to surrender on behalf of a fighter who is too stubborn to give up but who is suffering unacceptable harm. Alternatively, the referee may stop a fight for various reasons. In a sporting bout, intervention is normally a matter of fighter safety and there are rules in place to govern this. As with tapping out or submitting in any similar manner, submitting in a sport bout is final; the fight is over and there is a clear winner.

In a self-defense context, intervention can take many forms, not all of them useful. A fight between two individuals can be greatly complicated by bystanders or friends trying to separate the fighters or assist them. It is not uncommon for someone to get hurt because a well-meaning bystander or girlfriend was swinging on their arm trying to drag them away.

Intervention can also take the form of security or police personnel arriving to deal with the incident, or passers-by deciding to join in. It is not

In a sporting context, intervention normally takes the form of a coach or referee halting proceedings. When the guy in charge says it's over, it's over. Things are less clear-cut on the street.

uncommon for totally uninvolved people to run up and kick someone who is fighting or even lying helpless on the ground. This possibility for random intervention makes street fights, especially those that go to the ground, something of a gamble.

However, it is possible to use the intervention of others as a tool to end a situation. One of the few times when it is worth applying a restraint in a self-defense situation is when assistance is readily available. If an assailant can be restrained and handed over to police or security personnel, or if your friends are available to quickly dissuade him from continuing the altercation, then restraint may be a reasonable option. Otherwise, it is probably not a good idea unless the opponent is not much of a threat. The last thing you need is to be entangled with one opponent, trying to apply a restraint, only to be hit by one of his friends.

Winning

It is easy to think of "winning" a fight in terms of a clear-cut victory, but this is usually the case only in sporting bouts. In a self-defense context, "winning" is a more nebulous thing. It is more about you than the opponent, inasmuch as your goal is more likely to be to prevent yourself (or someone you want to protect) from coming to harm. It is not all that important how you achieve this, and indeed, a situation that involved you knocking the other guy clean out but taking a few shots into the bargain might be considered less of a victory than one where you were able to talk him down and never exchanged blows.

Winning, as already noted, is a matter of ending the situation on the most favorable terms you can obtain. There are many routes to that goal. In a

*The "fence" is used by security profes-
sionals worldwide. It is essentially a
modified fighting stance designed to be
non-threatening but to keep potential
aggressors at bay while remaining ready
to react if necessary.*

*Often the psychological barrier of the
fence posture is enough to deter an
aggressor. If not, he can be pushed vigorously away with a firm command to
keep his distance.*

*Often, a potential aggressor can be
deterred in this manner. If he comes
back again after being pushed away,
he is clearly determined to fight and
must be dealt with accordingly.*

sporting bout you can win by knockout or submission, or by wearing the
opponent down until he cannot go on any longer. You may even be able
to induce him to do something that will get him disqualified, though this
is a fairly hollow sort of victory. In any case, a winner will be announced
so the situation is fairly clear-cut. In a self-defense situation, things are
more nebulous. Winning can be achieved by many of the same methods,
but there are victories to be won in other ways too. An opponent who is
dragged off by nightclub security, or who allows his friends to persuade
him that you are not worth it, will not trouble you any more so this can
be considered a victory.

    In short, it is necessary to understand what you are trying to achieve
in order to have the best chance of victory. In a sports bout your aim will
usually be to be declared the winner by the judges. In a self-defense context
your goal is more likely to be to avoid coming to serious harm. If that is
achieved by hurting the assailant, so be it, but knocking him out or whatever you must do to him is not the goal, it is merely an outcome. The goal
is to get home safely, and so long as you achieve this then you have won.

What Makes an Effective Fighter?

Several factors, usually in combination, can make a fighter effective. There is no single formula for success; two equally good fighters may have entirely different advantages. However, the single overriding factor is mental rather than physical. It has many different names—guts, sand, heart, willingness, and élan to name a few—but what they all allude to is fighting spirit, the will to win, or, in some cases, sheer desperation.

The adage that, "it's not the size of the dog in the fight, but the size of the fight in the dog" may be a bit trite, but it is true. A skilled fighter can be beaten by a drunk brawler who just keeps throwing haymakers; a determined assailant can be driven off by a small, weak person who refuses to give up.

That said, will power alone does not guarantee success. Rather, it makes it possible. Without that will to struggle on and keep fighting, to risk taking painful blows or possibly being seriously hurt, it is not possible to defeat any but the most feeble opponent. Lack of will, or fighting spirit, can rob a fighter of a win in another way too; they may be unwilling to do what is necessary to complete the victory.

Someone who is winning has less at stake than their opponent. For example, a fighter who has a dominant position and is struggling to apply

Many factors combine to create an effective fighter, but high on the list is a combination of good coaching and hours spent on the mat, learning what works and struggling through when everything goes wrong.

a submission, or an assailant who is hoping to deliver a beating, has less incentive to keep going in the face of determined resistance than their disadvantaged opponent. The aggressor in a street assault has the choice of being able to break off any time they like. The defender often does not have this luxury. Likewise, someone trying to resist a submission does not have the option just to let go, but a fighter who is trying to apply one does.

If the defender is struggling hard and causing pain, he may cause an insufficiently determined opponent to back off. A given amount of pain may be entirely ignored when a fighter's attention is focused on getting a choke off his throat, because there is a more urgent concern. However, it requires rather more determination to accept the same amount of pain when it is less necessary. A fighter who chooses to relinquish his submission attempt loses little if he retains a dominant position. He is still winning, so may choose to find a different avenue of attack if the present one is costing him too much.

This factor is equally important to sporting and self-defense fighters. On the street, an assailant may decide that you are too much trouble. In the ring, it is sometimes possible to get out of a desperate situation by making the price tag for finishing you off a bit too high. Conversely, it is possible to lose a fight because you were not willing to accept the price of finishing it. An effective fighter weighs up the costs and the potential gains of his options—usually in a split second—and acts accordingly. He is willing to pay an affordable price to obtain a submission, but will not expose himself to the risk of unnecessary damage.

This ability to make rational decisions mid-fight is another hallmark of the effective fighter. It is possible to win by blindly bulling through, a method that works well enough for many aggressive drunks. However, a skilled fighter can exploit an opponent who over-commits to the attack,

It is essential to have the mental strength to deal with setbacks and the patience to get the opponent under control, even while he's hurting you. Then you can start working to improve your position, which might be a long and painful process.

and a tough one can often win simply by surviving long enough for the attacker to tire himself out with his constant assault.

A more rational opponent chooses his moment and makes the most of his opportunities with appropriate techniques. If a given avenue of attack is not working, he switches to another. He may set up a chosen attack by doing something else, for example throwing punches at the head to draw the opponent's attention upwards before launching a low takedown. If he spots that his opponent has a habit of doing a certain thing, he will find a way to exploit it.

The will to fight and win, and the ability to think quickly even under the stress of combat, can be summed up as the ability to function in the fight environment. Without this, there is a tendency to either fold up under pressure or to resort to blind, repetitive attacks, which may not be the best option under the circumstances. A fighter who can function effectively in combat can make the most of the tools at his disposal— but he still needs to have some.

Everyone has some combat "tools" of course. Kicking, screaming, biting, and scratching can be enough to deter or drive off an attacker, and an instinctive haymaker punch can drop him in his tracks. However, better tools are more effective. It goes without saying that well set up takedowns, properly executed punches that deliver maximum force and submissions applied from a strong position are far more likely to succeed than desperate flailing.

It is better to have a small selection of "tools," i.e. techniques, that are simple and easy to use, and to practice them until they can be delivered effectively under various circumstances, than to collect dozens of complex and impressive techniques that may or may not be much use. There is nothing wrong with knowing a dozen clever variations on the guillotine choke, but it is more important to have a basic, vanilla-flavor version that can be quickly applied when the opportunity arises.

Vast technical knowledge is an advantage of course, but application is far more important. The choke you apply may not be the best possible version but once it is on the opponent has to deal with it. That benefits you more than trying for a technically impressive variant and perhaps failing to achieve anything at all.

There are other advantages that a fighter can have. These include a superior understanding of tactics, better fitness, and of course size and strength. However, none of it matters if the fighter fails at the first hurdle —the ability to function in a fight environment. Adequate training will provide skills and improved fitness, probably along with a reasonable understanding of tactics. Good training, on the other hand, will tie it all together into a highly effective package and enable the fighter to keep his head under pressure. This in turn enables him to make best use of the advantages he possesses.

In summary, what makes a fighter effective is the possession of workable techniques and the physical ability to use them, the fitness to keep fighting long enough to win, and sufficient familiarity with what might happen to choose a suitable response to any given situation, all tied together by the ability to keep evaluating the situation and formulating strategy accordingly. Driven by a strong will to win, this package is formidable indeed.

It is, however, a package, and must be developed as one. Simply improving fitness or developing technical skill in isolation may not be enough. An understanding of tactics is only valid if the fighter is able to think rationally in combat and make use of his knowledge; otherwise it will only be useful for figuring out why defeat occurred. The goal that should underpin all forms of training is the creation of an effective fighter rather than the development of a single asset or technique.

No amount of fighting skills are worth anything unless you are willing to use them to harm someone. Some people find that harder than others, so an important part of your training is to build that willingness to fight and win.

CHAPTER 2

Functioning in the Fight Environment

The Fight Environment

The "fight environment" is a term used to refer to the various factors surrounding a physical confrontation. These factors are partly physical, partly psychological, and party environmental. An understanding of the fight environment is necessary for any serious attempt at preparation, and helps avoid unnecessarily losing a fight.

Many people think that training martial arts techniques is enough to guarantee victory over a less skilled opponent, but the reality is that technique is only a part of the puzzle. No amount of skill or physical prowess is of any use if the fighter folds under pressure or fails to make effective use of his abilities.

Nothing ever goes according to plan against a resistant opponent, so you need to train with "aliveness" to prepare you for the chaos that you will encounter when fighting anyone who isn't a pushover.

Techniques that seem straightforward in a martial arts class can become very difficult when attempted against a resistant opponent or under severe stress, so training must not only give the fighter the tools he (or she) needs to win a fight, it must also prepare the fighter to function in the fight environment. Good preparation includes all three dimensions—technical, physical, and psychological—and addresses the most likely situations a prospective fighter may find himself in.

The first question that has to be asked is: what is the fighter training goals? There are strong parallels between the sporting environment and "street" self-defense, but there are also significant differences. Even within the sporting arena, there are different kinds of competition and the fighter needs to be familiar with the characteristics of each. Last-minute ringside questions about whether kneeing from the clinch is permitted in this event are the hallmark of the unprepared (or perhaps just forgetful) fighter.

It is always necessary to consider environmental factors. For the sport fighter, the question is generally whether the bout is to take place on mats, in a ring, or a cage. This can be important—being slammed or taken down hard on a cage floor may be an unpleasant surprise for the fighter used to training on good mats, and surprises are best avoided. Tactical use of the ring or cage can also bring benefits to those who know how to do it or how to deal with those who do.

For the more general martial artist, perhaps training for self-defense, it is not really possible to predict where an incident might take place. Training needs to take account of the possibility of confined spaces, passing traffic,

Focus pads (some people call them hook-and-jab pads) are an essential and versatile training aid. The can be used to train many different techniques, but it is essential that the pad-holder knows how to absorb the bigger strikes if injuries are to be avoided.

Focus pads are most commonly used to train hand strikes, for which they are ideal. Wearing heavy gloves for pad drills has the added benefit of building the muscular endurance necessary to keep your hands up during a long fight.

uneven or slippery ground, poor lighting and so forth. The principles of effective combat are the same, but some techniques are simply not appropriate to certain environments. For example, most kicks are impossible to deliver in the aisle of a train or bus. This is not to say that a martial artist needs to undergo specific training in every possible environment, but he needs a broad range of techniques and the ability to decide what is appropriate in any given environment.

A fighter who is training for a sport fight knows when the event will take place, and what the rules will be. He knows that he will not suddenly be attacked with a weapon or by his opponent's friends. He also knows that the bout will be matched for weight. It will be timed and a referee and judges will impose a binding decision about who won. On the down side, he knows that he is facing a trained and skilled opponent, and he will have the added stress of doing it in front of an audience and possibly television cameras.

Knowing when and where the bout will take place and what the rules are being used enables the sport fighter to tailor his training to the environment. He can focus on tactics and techniques for dealing with a single opponent, and can bring his fitness to a peak at the right time. He may even be able to tailor his training to give him an advantage over a known opponent or to give the judges what they are looking for in order to win on a decision.

Conversely, when training more generally or for self-defense, we do not know when (or even if) a fight will occur. We cannot predict where it will be, nor who against. Numbers and weapons may play a part. Training must be tailored to dealing with an unpredictable situation and should include

When using focus pads to train low kicks, it is important to brace the pad against your leg. Even so, it is not really possible to take a pull-power kick on the pad, so this method is normally used for fairly light technical training.

Thai Pads are arguably a better option for all-round training, though they are more expensive than focus pads.

some common-sense conflict-avoidance or conflict-management skills to avoid unnecessary fights.

The single biggest difference between the "street" and the sporting arena is the uncertainty that prevails on the street. A sport fighter knows that his opponent has come to fight him. Someone confronted with an aggressive individual cannot know for sure whether the prospective opponent really wants a fight or is simply "posturing" for reasons that presumably make sense to him. This uncertainty can cause hesitation, and is exploited by those experienced in street violence.

A "street" aggressor may try to strike by surprise, perhaps by blindsiding the victim or by using deception to get close enough for a sudden assault. Innocuous sounding questions about the time or asking for a cigarette are common deceptions. Alternatively, a prospective assailant may test the waters by behaving aggressively, swearing, shouting, and pushing the victim. If he gets a response that makes him think he can win, he may escalate the level of violence. If he doesn't like the response he may instead choose to back off.

It is worth noting that although the build-up is different, once a fight begins the same principles apply to both sport and street fighting. Good training will prepare the fighter for the fight environment and enable him to keep his head under stress, both during the build-up to a fight and during it. A fighter who can handle the physical shock of being hit but who is taken out of the game by his reaction will be defeated as surely as one who is simply knocked out.

In a "flash drill" the pad holder offers the fighter a variety of targets, forcing him to react quickly with an appropriate strike. The fighter must be ready for anything rather than falling into comfortable habits.

A kick shield can absorb a full-power kick, though this is not always a pleasant experience for whoever is holding it. It is tempting to hold the pad away from your body, but this can result in injury. Keep the shield in tight and just accept that training sometimes hurts.

In-fight stress can also cause fighters to abandon their training and resort to brute force or wild swings, or to fight in a predictable manner that is easy to deal with. A fighter who keeps his head can often see opportunities and read his opponent's intentions. One who is badly rattled will miss obvious openings and let his opponent recover from mistakes instead of exploiting them.

This is a vital facet of all forms of fight training; the fighter must be properly prepared to not only perform techniques; he (or she) must also be able to keep a clear head and make quick decisions about what to do. It is this ability to function in the fight environment that separates an effective fighter from someone who can merely hit hard or perform good techniques.

In order that training can be realistic, focus pads should be used to provide a reasonable facsimile of a human target rather than simply being held up...

... that way strikes can be trained the same way they will be thrown in a fight.

Nobody's head is three feet wide...

... so the pads should be kept together rather than being allowed to drift apart as the strikes come in.

The pad-holder needs to shift quickly and crisply as the striker runs through a combination...

... offering the right target at the right time.

Good pad-setting is something of an art form....

... and is as much a part of good training as throwing the strikes themselves.

The Psychological Dimension

One of history's greatest generals commented that the "moral" (i.e. psychological) aspect was three times as important as the physical. He was talking about warfare, but the principles of personal combat are very similar. A relatively poor fighter who is willing to hold his ground and do his best will usually beat a half-hearted but more skilled opponent. Where the fighters are well matched, then psychological factors will usually decide the bout.

This fact has been known for centuries, and is understood on an instinctive level by most people. Generally speaking, many "street" aggressors will use threats and minor physical violence like grabbing and pushing to try to achieve dominance over their opponent. Some sport fighters do much the same thing with pre-fight intimidation, displays of prowess while entering the ring, trash talk to the cameras before the show, and so forth. In both cases, a fighter who is excessively fearful of the opponent will be dominated and has little chance of winning.

It is important that a fighter be trained to deal with these attempts to defeat him psychologically. Confidence is the best tool for countering intimidation, and this is built through good training. A fighter who is regularly tested and can meet the challenges put in front of him develops a habit of winning, and this confidence in his abilities will help him overcome the stress and uncertainty of the fight environment.

If a fighter is going to perform in front of an audience, then he needs to be prepared for this. He needs to be able to either forget about the onlookers and focus on his opponent, or to be able to accept that he is being watched and not become self-conscious. One way to achieve this is to train where outsiders can see from time to time, or to point out to the fighter that he is being watched while he trains whenever someone goes by. Familiarity with an audience can reduce the stress of fight night. So can being an inveterate show-off, but not every fighter has the sort of personality that relishes an audience.

"Stress inoculation" is a useful technique for training both self-defense and sport fighting. Scenario work is used by many self-defense trainers, and can benefit the sport fighter too. One common scenario is to restrict the fighter to responding only if the "aggressor" launches an actual attack. The aggressor (often using body armor and boxing gloves) then postures aggressively, shouts threats and abuse at the fighter, and tries to intimidate him.

Competition bouts are normally matched for skill, experience, and body mass, but there's a lot to be said for training against people who are bigger, stronger, and infinitely more scary than you are. If you can handle battling monsters then the prospect of fighting a well-matched opponent should not disturb you much.

Do not underestimate the psychological dimension. A wild swing should be easy to see coming and avoid or counter, but the berserk intent of the attacker can sometimes cause a fighter to freeze and get hit. Good training will change your reaction from "Help! He's trying to hurt me!" to "Oh, look, a haymaker. Is that all you've got?"

The fighter must make an intelligent choice under stress to respond effectively if and when an attack occurs, or to observe what the aggressor is doing and make a "no-shoot" decision if he does not attack.

There are many variations on this theme. The "aggressor" can make sudden attacks which may not be all that physically painful but look intimidating (e.g. big wild swings, grabbing the fighter and shaking or shoving him, and so forth), all of which forces the fighter to try to respond intelligently despite the stress. These techniques are used extensively by law enforcement trainers and reality-based self-defense instructors, but can also be applied to the sport fighter's training. Being able to deal with aggression without becoming intimidated is a vital part of fight preparation.

More conventional approaches like sparring or rolling can also be used for the same purpose, of course. Sparring can be set up to put the fighter under extreme pressure, perhaps by using a rotation of fresh opponents with no break for the fighter. As he becomes more tired, his will is eroded and his determination to win will be sorely tested. It is important not to push the fighter too far, but used with care this approach can build fighting spirit.

One useful trick is to mess with the fighter's expectations. Tell him that he is doing three 1-minute rounds with fresh opponents, then keep going after the three. Or allow the bouts to run on for more than the expected minute. The lesson the fighter needs to learn (more accurately, his subconscious needs to learn) is that "it's not over until it's over." Too many fighters let go towards the end of a bout or ease up when they think they've done enough to win. The fighter has to be able to keep at it until the end, or maybe to get back into the fight when his flagging opponent (who may think he's won and be easing up) gives him an opportunity.

If you lose your head, you'll lose the fight. A good fighter is capable of acting intelligently even when things go wrong. Gary (on top) is bigger and stronger and I've just been taken down pretty hard.

To prevent matters getting any worse for me, I control Gary's head and try to hook one of his legs. If I can prevent him from transitioning to a fully dominant position, I'll give myself a chance to improve the situation.

The fight for position begins in earnest. Gary pushes down on my shoulder to break my grip on his head as he tries to move around to the side.

He succeeds in freeing his head, but I've still got control of his leg. At this moment, that's about the only thing between me and being submitted, and we both know it. On the plus side I've avoided being quickly beaten, which means that things are bad but I'm still in the fight... and as long as I'm in the fight then I'll be trying to win it.

The psychological dimension must be used with care to avoid doing more harm than good, but mental conditioning can be built into the fighter's training at every level. Fitness work, even technical drills can be set up to build the habit of pushing on through to the end, even when things are bad. This is important, because nothing ever goes according to plan and some-times the margin between defeat and victory is simply the fighter's own willingness to keep at it when someone else might have given up.

How to Attack the Human Body

The human body is a marvelous thing; incredibly robust in some ways yet vulnerable in others. Race drivers have been seen to climb out of the wreckage of a 200-mph crash, kick a tire in disgust, and walk away... and yet people have died from slipping in the shower. Thus an attack can be devastating if it hits the right spot, or merely annoying if the aim is off. Most of the "pressure point" techniques taught in martial arts are unworkable in a real fight, as it is difficult to hit just the right spot. So as a rule, it is better to strike at large targets that will get you at least some benefit, rather than to try for that perfect one-shot knockout and risk achieving nothing.

It is not usually possible to attack small areas of the body with great precision in the chaos of a fight, though precision can be achieved if a measure of control can be exerted over the opponent. Although most wrist-catching martial arts techniques are virtually useless against an opponent who is moving around and throwing punches, it is possible to apply a Kimura, a locking technique that requires the fighter to hold his opponent's wrist. Is this a contradiction? Not really.

The answer, obviously, is that once the opponent is under control, e.g. is held or pushed up against something, then it becomes easier to apply precise techniques. A clean hit to the jaw may well drop an opponent and win the bout by knockout, but landing that shot is problematic. Most fighters have to settle for hitting hard to the head in general. You might get lucky, hit "the button" and end the matter then and there, but if not then each blow will still rattle the opponent and wear him down.

Let us not forget that every time you hurt an opponent's body, you also attack his will to win the fight. Pain, fatigue, disorientation from repeated blows to the head, and the general feeling of being overmatched can cause an opponent to "lose the fight in his head" and give up or at least start trying not to lose rather than fighting to win. Once he is defensive, he is well on the way to defeat.

There are only so many ways to attack an opponent. These include direct impact (e.g. strikes, knees and kicks), secondary impact (e.g. throws and takedowns that cause the opponent to land hard), joint locks, and chokes/strangles.

Direct Impact

In a sport fight, the rules will dictate what is permitted, for example it may not be legal to knee to the head or to strike the head while the opponent is on the ground. Outside the sporting arena, there are no rules for this sort of thing, but actions must be lawful to avoid criminal charges. This is covered in the next section.

It is generally a bad idea to strike hard targets (e.g. the head) with fists unless you are wearing gloves. Even then, injuries to the hands are not uncommon. For the "street," the head is best attacked with open hands (e.g. palm strikes) or hammerfists. However, a punch that drops an assailant and prevents you from being seriously harmed is still a "win" even if your hand is damaged. A properly formed, tight fist will help prevent damage to the hand but the risk is always present. With gloves, even light MMA gloves, the hazards are significantly reduced.

The head is most definitely the primary target for direct impact techniques. Even a glancing head strike can cause "brain shake" that can disorient an opponent or knock him out. There is also the possibility of inflicting cuts, causing eyes to swell shut, and so forth. Injuries may cause a sport bout to be halted on medical grounds or simply reduce an opponent's performance.

It has been wisely said that: "Head shots hurt. Body shots hurt the whole fight." A good body shot might put the opponent down, so badly winded or hurt that he simply cannot carry on, but even if it does not, blows to the body can weaken the opponent in various ways. Most movements use the muscles of the body, and strikes can weaken these. The most important effect is on breathing. Even if he is not put down by a body shot, an opponent will be feeling it for a good while and every time he takes a breath. Body shots thus reduce his ability to get air in, and that translates to reduced performance.

Attacks to the arms are of limited value at best, but the legs are a good target. Many fighters condition the outer part of their thighs and can take a solid kick or two, but you can chop down the toughest fighter eventually.

Punches are not thrown "to" the target, they are thrown "through" and out the back. A pad or bag should dent or crumple under a properly delivered strike.

Knee strikes are best thrown from a clinch, and are almost always thrown from the trailing leg for maximum impact.

A knee strike may or may not disable the opponent, but it will certainly weaken him and enable a follow-up attack to be made.

Kicks to the inside of the leg are often more effective as it is hard to condition these areas. Either way, leg kicks can cause an opponent to stagger even if he is not seriously hurt, and while he's staggering, he's not hitting you.

As a general rule, forget about flashy techniques like spinning kicks and backfists, and stick to basic, vanilla-flavor pounding. Attacking the head, body and legs allows you to keep the opponent guessing and to find an opening (or make one) if he's got a good defense. Leg or body shots may pull the opponent's guard down (or crumple him up, which can have the same effect), allowing a clear shot at the head.

Hand strikes are normally thrown at the head and body. Straight-on hand strikes to the body are less effective than shots that come in from the side, ideally into the diaphragm or kidney regions. Striking slightly upwards under the ribs works better than hitting downwards.

Kicks are best thrown at the legs and the body. Head kicks are awesomely potent when they land but they need to be set up and can compromise your balance. They can be a useful tool for MMA but are best added after you have a solid base of more widely useful techniques.

Knees and elbows are the premier striking tools for demolishing an opponent. They are best used from a clinch or another hold rather than "free" and require you to be at close quarters. Knee strikes will normally target the body or legs, but you can pull an opponent's head down onto a knee if you can get him under control. Elbows are normally thrown to the head but can target any other area within reach, especially on the ground.

An effective fighter makes good use of his environment. Something as simple as a good hard push becomes a lot more potent when you slam the opponent into something...

... and not only does it hurt, but it can open up the opponent for strikes if his arms splay out when he hits the wall.

Big throws are hard to pull off against a serious opponent, so it's not worth training with them until your basic skills improve. But that's a long, long fall...

... and a landing that might end the fight then and there.

Secondary Impact

A lot of the takedowns taught in martial arts are, to a great extent, misused. They are often used simply as a means to get the opponent on the ground so that he can be attacked there. This is useful, but it passes up on two opportunities to harm the opponent. The first is in the performance of the takedown itself; often it is possible to deliver a strike while grabbing the opponent or forcing him to fall. Taking advantage of every chance to hurt or harm the opponent is always a good idea.

The other opportunity is of course the chance to slam the opponent into the ground as hard as possible. It may not be necessary to follow up with ground techniques if your takedown is powerful enough, but even if it is not then a hard impact will prevent the opponent from defending very effectively for a moment and allow you to gain a more dominant position. On the street, it is usually preferable to dump an assailant hard and use this an opportunity to leave the scene than to follow him to the ground, but if you do end up following him down a hard takedown will gain you a significant advantage.

Throws differ from takedowns mainly in their definition. A takedown causes the opponent to fall; a throw requires that you bear his weight for an instant. Thus a hip throw, where you carry the opponent's weight on your back for a moment, is by definition a throw while a single-leg takedown, which breaks his balance and then takes away a leg causing him to fall, is a takedown. Throws are generally more damaging; takedowns are more accessible. It is better to concentrate on simple takedowns at first, adding throws only when you are very skilled.

Joint Locks

It is possible to attack any joint, though some are difficult to get at or achieve poor results so it can be ignored. There are three possible reasons to attack joints; to break or destroy the joint, to obtain a submission (tap out) by pain and the threat of destroying the joint, or to put the opponent where you want him and keep him there while you do whatever you want to do next.

It is worth bearing in mind that all techniques taught as submissions are in fact ways to wreck a joint, and are simply scaled back to the point where they can be used safely. This cuts both ways—it means that if you need to disable someone in order to defend yourself, the same technique can be used to break a joint as to obtain a tap, and it also means that excessive force in training or competition can result in injuries that may never heal properly.

Locking a joint simply means making it do something it is not designed to do, usually by forcing it against its normal range of motion. While finger and wrist locks are occasionally useful, they are difficult to obtain and generally less effective than many martial artists imagine. Small-joint manipulations are usually banned in competition, in any case. Neck cranks are also illegal in many competitions, though they are sometimes an accidental by-product of an attempt at a choke.

Joint locking techniques are often used for control and restraint by security professionals. The threat to a joint can be used to force compliance or put a subject where you want him.

Wrist locks can seem effective in class, but are virtually impossible to apply in a serious fight.

Leg locks affecting the ankle and knee can be very effective, but to get them you have to control an opponent's legs (which tend to be powerful) with your arms, and to be in a position to do so. Leg locks are thus a body of technique to be added once you have a good set of basic techniques that are more generally useful.

An Achilles' tendon lock is a useful technique, but only under fairly specific circumstances. It's better to concentrate on more generally-applicable techniques first, and then add more specialized material later.

That leaves elbow and shoulder locks. These are the staple submissions used in MMA and are highly useful for self-defense. An opponent who cannot use his arm cannot hit you with it. Arms are also relatively easy to grab in a fight, since opponents often send them flying towards you or try to grab you with them. All of the locking techniques in this volume attack the arms.

It is important to note one critical difference between "street" and "sport" environments. Submission in a sporting bout tends to be the end of the matter, but in a self-defense context there is no reason to suppose that the opponent will not come back for another go immediately upon being released from a submission hold.

For this reason, it is wise to be judicious in the use of submissions. If you judge that the situation merits it, it is more effective to use a joint lock to cause damage then let go and see if the opponent still wants to fight with a broken arm. Alternatively, many joint locks and choke holds can be used to control an opponent, for example putting him where he can be more effectively struck, or slamming him into a wall or the floor.

Chokes and Strangles

These two terms are often used interchangeably. If it is necessary to differentiate, a "choke" is primarily targeted at the windpipe and cuts off the

Something as simple as dropping weight onto an arm across the opponent's throat can restrict his breathing and keep him pinned. This won't win the fight but it'll help control the opponent while a more solid position is established.

A choke-hold can be an effective restraint, or can be used to render an opponent unconscious. If left on too long, a choke or strangle will kill. Safety in training and care in actual use is vital.

air supply, while a "strangle" cuts off the blood supply to the brain at the carotid arteries. In practice, many techniques are a bit of both.

Chokes are frightening and hugely unpleasant but can take a while to have any real effect, during which time the opponent will often struggle violently. A partial choke, which is not enough to cause an opponent so submit, can still be useful. It controls his head, and where his head goes, the rest of him goes—if not then something has gone terribly wrong! More importantly, it restricts his breathing and wears him down, and, of course, it is frightening and will erode his will to win.

A strangle is more insidious. Many people (especially untrained or poorly trained fighters) will not necessarily realize what is happening and may not know the extent of their danger. A properly applied strangle (or "sleeper hold") can render the opponent unconscious in a few seconds, and will kill if kept on for much longer. Safety is of paramount importance when training these techniques, and care needs to be used when applying them in actual combat.

Most chokes and strangles are not 100% "on" and can be resisted or escaped from. However, common sense suggests that it is wise to tap out before you are in serious danger—by all means resist if the technique is not fully applied, but struggling until you pass out is dangerous and ultimately pointless.

Legal Considerations

Many of the things that you might do in the course of an MMA bout are illegal elsewhere, but doing them in a properly licensed sporting event makes the violence acceptable, providing the fighters remain within the rules and referees keep matters under proper control. Thus if you abide by the rules of a sporting event (the same applies in training) then you do not need to worry about legal considerations. Fighters do get injured, but provided the event is properly insured and licensed then there should be no legal complications.

Insurance is an important issue for training and competing. As well as being a legal requirement, it is important in case of an accident, to cover lost income from time off work and the like. Insurance to train, to coach, and to run an event are all different areas, with varying costs depending on what is being done. It is not very difficult to obtain insurance to teach most martial arts, including MMA (assuming you are qualified to do so), providing it is not for competition, i.e. if MMA is being taught as if it was a martial art like any other, then the insurance situation is not very different than that for karate or judo.

Insurance to train a fighter for competition is more expensive as the risks are greater. It may be tempting not to bother with it, but this leaves the people involved open to a variety of risks; anyone serious about training to fight should be properly insured.

For self-defense, the law is an important factor. Some martial arts teach techniques that can be quite extreme without properly briefing their students on the use of force within the law. This is irresponsible; a defense against an assault, which lands you in jail, is not really a "win."

The law varies from one area to another, but in general the principles tend to be the same: you are permitted to use force to protect yourself or someone else, to prevent or stop a crime, and to protect property. But the force you use must be reasonable and necessary.

There is no set response to any given threat; the question is simply whether or not what you did was reasonable under the circumstances. So if you did not want to fight and did not seek conflict, and what you did to protect yourself seems reasonable, then the law is on your side.

The question of what is "reasonable force" is a broad and complex one. For example, is it reasonable to hit an assailant twelve times? The answer is of course "it depends." Supposing you hit him eleven times and he was still trying to harm you… and number twelve stopped him. Was the twelfth blow necessary? Looks that way, so it's reasonable.

On the other hand, supposing he folded up after the second one and you delivered a sound beating. What then? However much the bad guy may have deserved the other ten shots, once he was no longer a threat to you then your actions would no longer constitute self-defense and you would risk prosecution.

There is some leeway here of course. Private citizens are not expected to be able to judge exactly what level of force is necessary to stop a given assailant, so you would not normally be sent to jail for one extra blow that at the time seemed to be necessary. Certain actions are governed by specific laws in some areas, however. These include stamping on or kicking a downed opponent, strangling and the like. It is worth looking into your local laws regarding self-defense, but there is a general rule that applies in most localities:

Assuming you didn't start the incident and were not looking for trouble, and you only did what you had to, then your actions should be legal as self-defense.

If, after an incident, you were asked "did you really need to do that?" and you can truthfully reply that yes, you did... and you can explain why to the satisfaction of a sensible person, then your actions will normally be considered self-defense within the law. To put that another way: if nobody can suggest a workable alternative to what you did, then it will be obvious that you had no choice... and nobody expects you to be a victim.

A simple rule for understanding self-defense law is: if the opponent is still a threat to you, you may use as much force as is necessary to stop him. Stomping all over a helpless opponent does not constitute self-defense... no matter how much he deserves it.

CHAPTER 3

Fighting Principles

Range and Distance

The concepts of range and distance in a fight are open to all manner of interpretations, most of which are as valid as any other. For our purposes, "range" is significant because it delineates what you can do, while "distance" is primarily important because it affects the time you have available to make an attack or to react to one.

Range

We need consider only four "ranges" in combat, and they need not be precisely defined. In this context, range can be considered to be a situation rather than a precise measurement of exactly how far the fighters are apart. Range is primarily significant because it allows us to predict what sort of threats are likely, and to know which techniques are most likely to work. It is not necessary to split hairs about precise distances; what matters is the options open to the fighters.

- **Out:** The fighters are so far apart that neither can do anything to the other without making a significant movement first. Any attack launched from this far away has virtually zero chance of success providing the opponent is on the ball. It is possible to get caught out by an opponent who runs in from the other side of the cage, but it is very, very rare.
- **Open:** The fighters are close enough that an attack can be launched with a decent chance of success, perhaps requiring a step or a shoot to bring the attack into range. There is no need to distinguish between kicking and striking range; what matters is that the opponent is close enough to be a threat but is not in physical contact. Most attacks from open range are strikes and kicks, but a takedown attempt can be made using a shoot or other forward movement, and some fighters will attempt to close in and establish a grip.

The fighters are "out," i.e. fairly far apart, and can only hit one another with a very obvious movement. A long kick thrown from here might land, but the opponent will have plenty of time to react.

The range is "open," i.e. the fighters are close enough to hit one another without moving too far and the full range of options are open to both. A fast attack at this range has a good chance of landing before the opponent can react. This is a dangerous place; don't be at this range unless you intend to attack immediately.

- **Clinch:** The fighters are upright and in physical contact. A clinch or other grappling is almost inevitable at this range, even when the fighters are pure strikers (boxers). Striking options are somewhat limited—most kicks and many hand strikes are impossible—but various close-quarters strikes are possible, along with the full range of grappling and takedown attempts.

The fighters have hold of one another and are clinched up. Ironically this is a safer place to be in many ways than "open" range, as the opponent's options are limited and it is possible to feel the movement that sets up an attack.

The fight is going to the ground. One fighter is already down and the other is likely to follow him or be pulled down.

- **Down:** The fighters are on the ground. Most standup strikes are, obviously, impossible. The groundfighting environment is significantly different to all other ranges, though many principles are shared with the clinch. A fighter who lacks at least a basic understanding of the specialist skills of groundfighting is at a severe disadvantage on the ground.

Distance

Distance is of secondary importance compared to range, but can still be significant. Various attacks have a differing reach depending upon the opponent's height, skill, and speed. One fighter might be able to reach you with a punch at a distance where another can only land a kick; this matters at open range, but at clinch range it is largely irrelevant.

Distance relates directly to time. The further away an opponent is, the longer it will take an attack to cross the distance between you. Exactly how long depends on many factors, but the important thing is that at very short distances you will simply not have time to react. Conversely, some techniques require a certain amount of distance to be effective. A roundhouse kick has to have room to develop; closing the distance will weaken the kick and opening it may make it miss entirely.

Distance is just as important on the ground as standing up. If you are tightly gripped against your opponent, it is difficult for either of you to make any effective attacks. You will need to make room for your attack, just as you would have to close in if you were too far out.

Keith (left) has set up a front kick from the correct distance, and has no trouble sinking it into Mark's (right) chest.

This time, Keith commits to his kick too early...

... allowing Mark to move back out of reach.

The kick falls well short, possibly exposing Keith to a counterattack.

Using Range and Distance

Effective control of range and distance is a highly useful tool. You can change the range of the fight to suit your skills and to limit the opponent's options. Alternatively, you might use distance in a more subtle manner. For example, you might choose to hover close to the outside of your opponent's reach, trying to tempt him into a long attack that you will have plenty of time to deal with. Or you might close him down to prevent a kick landing. On the ground you might hug in close from the mount, popping up to drop a couple of shots in before closing in tight to avoid any counter or reversal attempt.

As a rule, you are safest either right out or right in. Anywhere in between, and you are open to attack. Of course, you can also launch an attack of

Closing the distance can be used offensively or defensively. If you get tagged, the worst thing that you can do is stagger back or remain at your opponent's best striking distance. Instead, cover your head and "crash in," closing the distance to shut down his strikes while you recover.

your own, but always remember that if you're close enough to attack then so is the opponent. There is an exception to this; if you have very good mobility and/or reach, you can remain at what amounts to his "out" range while you are at the outer fringe of your "open'"range. This requires very fine judgement but is a technique favored by tall kickers and highly mobile fighters.

The only reason for being close enough to attack (and therefore, to be attacked) is because you intend to attack or make the opponent think you are about to attack. If you want to back off a bit, then back off far enough that you are "out." The opponent will have to expend a lot of energy to attack you and you'll have time to react. Staying closer leaves you open to attack at a time when you might think you are safe.

Constantly changing the distance will keep an opponent guessing. Changing the range may throw his plans into disarray as he tries to set up a clinch and takedown only to find that you are suddenly too far away. Conversely, be aware of attempts by the opponent to dictate the range. If he is best at a given range then you need to beware of spending too much time there.

Striking and Grappling

The difference between striking and grappling is an artificial one. Some techniques are clearly one or the other—a roundhouse kick is a strike and an arm bar is a grappling technique, for example. However, do not be trapped into thinking of striking and grappling as separate things. They are both highly useful in the right context, and there is a lot of crossover.

If you clinch an opponent and knee him, or take him down for ground-and-pound, are you striking or grappling? The answer is that it doesn't

One problem with always training grappling or striking in isolation is that you can develop blind spots. As I fixate too much on passing my opponent's guard, I'm just asking for a punch in the side of the head.

Something as simple as pushing an arm down can prevent the opponent from striking you as you move into a better position. A good fighter is aware of his opponent's options and takes action to limit them.

matter. You're fighting. And hopefully, winning. Do not worry excessively about what is grappling and what is striking unless you are in a situation where one is not permitted in the rules. In both MMA and self-defense, you would be wise to use all your tools rather than just one type. There is nothing wrong with setting up a submission by striking or kneeing your opponent, or holding him while you deliver close-range strikes.

Many fighters are predominantly strikers or grapplers, but for all-round effectiveness it is necessary to be at least somewhat skilled in both areas. By all means, drill striking and grappling separately most of the time, but you will need to spend at least some of your training time on situations where both are permitted. This will help you avoid fixating on one or the other, instead using both grappling and striking techniques to advance your position.

Mixed training will also help you avoid falling victim to novice mistakes, like leaving yourself wide open to an attack you haven't experienced. You will almost certainly prefer to fight in your strongest style, and should angle your training accordingly, but do not neglect the areas you do not like so much. No matter how good your grappling skills might be, for example, they are worthless if you are knocked out by a punch before you can establish a good position. Even if your skills in one area are not enough to obtain a finish, they can help you survive long enough (and get out of bad situations) to use your main skills.

Stance and Guard

There are many different fighting arts, and most of them use some variation on a basic fighter's stance. However, the whole stance concept is often misunderstood. It is posture (or body structure) rather than any specific stance that is important. Slight variations on the basic stances are no problem so long as the fighter is well positioned to do what he needs to do.

Do not focus on any one specific part of the opponent. Instead rest your gaze roughly on the upper chest, around the notch between the collarbones. Your peripheral vision will take in all of the opponent and will pick up his movements faster than if you stared at one part of him.

Some arts use stances geared to one particular style of combat. For example, judo players and wrestlers are not concerned about striking as this is not allowed in their art. Similarly, boxers do not need to worry about a stance that will resist takedowns well; the rules protect them better than any stance.

For the mixed martial artist or self-defense practitioner, the situation is less clear. An opponent could strike, kick, or grapple, and will probably try to do whichever the fighter's stance is least well prepared to defend against. Thus the most important component of a general-purpose fighting stance is flexibility.

No guard position or fighting stance is perfect for every application. What matters most is that you must be comfortable with your guard position and the options it offers.

So long as your guard position gives you a good range of defensive and offensive options, it will serve. Obsessing about a perfect stance is mainly relevant to non-fighting martial arts. We are more concerned about what you can do from your stance than how good it looks.

No fighting stance is a suit of armor; it will always be necessary to move in order to deal with an attack or to deliver one. So a stance should be considered as a starting point, a position that the fighter passes through on the way to doing something rather than a static position to be perfected and admired in a mirror.

As a general rule, hands should be up, guarding the head. Most "street" attackers will attack the head almost exclusively, often with wild swings, so a position protecting the head is wise. A slightly lower hand position makes sense in MMA, where a trained opponent might vary his attacks. But do remember that gravity makes it harder to raise your hands than to drop them to cover a low attack. Starting from a reasonably high position makes sense.

As a general rule, strikes are thrown and evaded from a relatively "light" stance, moving quickly with weight on the balls of the feet. Grappling attacks are dealt with (or launched) from a generally wider base. The ability to shift stance slightly to deal with what is happening is an important one.

Striker's Guard

Striker's guard is an excellent generic striking position. Normally your weak hand is forward, and your dominant hand and will be kept back in reserve. However, it is worth training from an opposite stance from time to time. You can't always guarantee where you'll put your foot down from a kick or stumble, so some familiarity with the opposite lead is useful as your skills develop.

The basic position is slightly more square on than a boxer might use, to enable kicks and grappling attacks. Movements tend to be quick and light, closing to launch strikes then moving back out of range to avoid retaliation, or evading counterattacks while staying in close. Feet will be turned in (the front one is often less turned in than the rear one) and the rear heel may or may not be cocked depending on what's comfortable for you. This is a good launch platform for strikes, but if you get kicked hard or grappled while you're up on your toes, it can be hard to avoid going down.

A striker's guard is fairly upright and mobile, strong hand back to protect the head. Center of gravity is relatively high, compared to a grappler's guard.

Grappler's Guard

With a wider foot position and lower center, this more square-on position is highly resistant to being taken down or unbalanced by a grappling attack. It is a good base to launch a grappling attack from, but it can be ponderous when moving or trying to strike. This position is also somewhat open to striking and kicking techniques.

A solid base is essential to grappling, which necessitates a wide, low stance. This can make it difficult to evade a strike, and makes it obvious that you expect to launch or receive a grappling attack.

In Between

Many fighters use a position that is somewhere in between the striker and grappler positions. This has the advantage of not giving away what you intend to do. A fairly wide, fairly square stance with a relatively low hand position is favored by many fighters. This is effective, but remember that the single most serious threat is a blow to the head (because it's the commonest attack and a single shot could take you out of the fight) so don't allow your hands to drop so low that you cannot protect your head.

Stance is, to a great extent, a personal thing and must be adapted to the circumstances (e.g. an opponent who is taller or shorter than you). What is important is that your stance is well balanced and allows you to move freely or to drop your weight to defend against a takedown attempt. And of course, a good stance is a starting point for what you want to do, not a goal in and of itself.

In all cases, a good stance has certain features:

- Reasonably wide foot position for stability in all directions. Shoulder width or a little wider is a good guide
- Well balanced and not flat-footed. Weight should be on the balls of the feet.
- Hands well placed to protect the head or deliver head strikes
- Chin tucked in and shoulder slightly raised to protect the jaw

Somewhere in between a pure grappling and pure striking stance is a comfortable position that gives you plenty of options and doesn't betray your intentions.

- Not excessively upright or hunched up
- Ready to move or to "drop" weight to deal with a grappling situation

Footwork and Positioning

The basic principle of all combat footwork is the push-shuffle. Shuffling means that your feet should not cross. Actually, some movements require that they do, but these are exceptions to the general rule. You are extremely vulnerable to being hit, taken down, or just pushed over with your feet crossed up, so this is something that should only happen when you have a specific reason for doing it.

The "push" part is the key to almost every footwork movement. Whichever direction you want to go, the other foot pushes you. You should never step with the lead foot then catch up with the rear one; this leaves you dangerously committed to the movement. Likewise, you should not stand up straight and simply walk about in a fight. You should start in a good stance and finish in one, and in between your movements should be precise and efficient.

Forward and Back

To step forward, "go light" on your front foot (i.e. start to lift it up) and drive forward by pushing through the back foot. A step should be no longer than your shoulder width. Bring the back foot up (don't drag it along the floor) to its natural position. You should now be in the same stance as when you started.

Backwards is the same in reverse. Lift up your rear foot and reach for the ground behind you, driving through your front foot. When the back foot reaches the ground, it acts as a brake. Bring the front foot to its natural position. Do not let your hands drop as you move!

From a neutral stance, push forward with the back foot...	*... step forward with the front foot, without lifting it up high...*	*... then bring the back foot up. Don't take an excessively long step; your back foot will end up more or less where the front one was.*

Drop-step

The drop-step is a variation on the standard forward shuffle, used to add weight to a strike or a push. It is performed much the same way as a forward shuffle, but your strike (or other technique) should connect as your front foot hits the ground, and with your weight committed behind it. You won't stagger forward if you execute the step right, but you will transfer maximum force into your opponent.

A drop-step is a big heavy step forward used to add power to a heavy punch or a push.

The aim is to land your shot while your weight is still dropping forward.

Stepping Through

This is an exception to the "don't cross your feet" rule. Your rear foot drives forward then steps through to switch leads. There are various reasons for doing this, such as a rear-leg push-kick. You an also step obliquely through to place yourself on an opponent's flank.

Circling

As a general rule, fighters will circle away from an opponent's power side (i.e. to their own right, away from his powerful right hand). This is relatively easy; step diagonally with your rear foot and push with your lead foot, then bring the lead foot up. Going the other way is only slightly more difficult; you will need to step to your left with your lead foot and then bring the rear foot across. Obviously, this is reversed if you are in a right lead.

Nobody really has an advantage here. All our "weapons" (punches, kicks, takedown attempts, and particularly vile insults) are aimed straight forward, and the opponent's guard is in the way.

Nate steps out to the side, away from my strong hand, and off the line of anything I might throw.

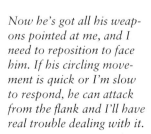

Now he's got all his weapons pointed at me, and I need to reposition to face him. If his circling movement is quick or I'm slow to respond, he can attack from the flank and I'll have real trouble dealing with it.

Positioning

Positioning is what makes the difference between a halfway successful technique and a truly effective one. Many groundfighting experts talk of "position before submission," meaning the need to put yourself where the technique has the best chance of success before attempting it, but in truth this does not just apply to groundfighting.

There are only two reasons for being where an opponent can grab or strike you—either because you are about to grab or strike him, or else you want him to try something. Drawing an attack in this manner can be extremely effective if it works, but it requires a great deal of skill and some luck. Once your skills reach an advanced level it may become an option but for now it is a risky prospect.

That leaves one reason for being within reach of the opponent: you want to do something to him right now! If you are not attacking or about to attack, stay out of reach. Use your mobility and footwork to stay away from him, or at least keep enough distance that any attack he makes will have to cover a lot of distance. Distance equates to time in this case; time to counter or defend.

Tactically, one good option is to keep moving around and making the opponent launch low-percentage, long attacks that are easy to defend against and will tire him out. But you can only do this for so long. At some point you'll have to take the fight to the opponent. Positioning is important here; some fighters will just bull in no matter what, but that often means wasting energy or leaving yourself open to a sucker-punch. You should instead make your attacks when you choose; position yourself to have a good chance to succeed, launch the attack and if it doesn't get you what you want, get back out. Staying close to the opponent after a failed attack risks being hit by an attack you won't have time to see coming.

While the fighters are apart, it is wise to circle, open and close distance, disguise your intentions and pick your moment. When you do go in, do so quickly but not blindly, and ideally do not just charge forward. One obvious option is to hit-move-hit again. For example, you might bang in a couple of punches then circle to your right before launching the next one. This puts you on the opponent's flank where his main striking weapons are not aimed at you. A shot across the jaw is an excellent knockout blow, while a side body shot is more effective than a frontal one in most cases.

Positioning is also vital to delivering an attack. If you are off balance or at the wrong distance then a strike will have little effect and a take-down attempt will be easily defended. Putting yourself or the opponent where your techniques will have the greatest effect is a skill that should be developed throughout training. Take note of the distance when doing pad

Attacking head-on gives the opponent too many defensive options. Mark (right) decides to reposition himself for a better opening.

Mark throws a big, heavy right hand to force Chris (left) to defend with a front cover...

... and circles while Chris can't see him, lining up a big right hand from the side.

It no longer matters that Chris is covered to the front; Mark isn't there any more. His straight right has a clear path to the target.

work; you'll realize that some strikes land harder than others; the distance must not be too long or too short. Learn the distances that optimize your attacks, and put yourself there before you throw them.

Energy is a precious commodity in a fight, but a little energy spent on positioning yourself well can save you loads more because you don't have to launch dozens of marginal attacks to get a result. Just as importantly, spoiling your opponent's attempts at positioning can prevent you being defeated.

Defeating Attacks

There are only so many ways to defeat an attack. The very best one is to be on the offensive all the time so that the opponent never gets a chance to do anything, but that is a bit optimistic. If you can force the opponent on the defensive by what you do in or before the fight (i.e. if he's intimidated by your reputation or obvious skills) then this does serve as an effective defense. An opponent who is overawed by you will not commit to attacks like someone who thinks he can beat you will, and that works to your advantage.

However, most of the time you'll face an opponent who is reasonably confident in his ability to defeat you. Even then, you can deter a lot of attacks by having a good guard up, using your mobility and generally showing him that you are likely to defend whatever he throws at you. An untrained person might come flailing in anyway (watch out for that!) but most skilled fighters will recognize that your defense is solid and will not waste effort on low-percentage attacks.

Thus by observing basic principles you can go a long way towards defeating most of the attacks that might otherwise be thrown at you. A good guard makes some angles of attack ineffective, a good stance and use of distance makes some takedown attempts pointless. So you can limit your opponent's actions… but you can't eliminate all of them. He will look for a way in, and when he thinks he's seen one he will attack. However, by limiting his options you improve the chances of a successful defense, since you know what's likely to be coming in and where.

However, do not forget that defense is only what you do when you're not attacking. Nobody ever won a fight by pure defense. So any defense you make should be part of a greater plan. Ideally your defense will be offensive. For example you might bob under a punch and come back up with one of your own, using your defensive movement to set up your attack. However, often it's necessary to accept that you're going to get hit, and your defense is simply a way of mitigating the damage to allow you to hand out more harm in return.

This is one important difference between point-sparring combat sports and "real" fighting (i.e. with contact). In a "points" context a defense is all or nothing—you either stop the attack completely or you get points scored against you. In a real combat situation things tend to be less clean-cut. For example, you might have to cover a punch but still take some of the force in order to get in and land a couple of your own. Two good ones as opposed to one partially defended one is a good exchange ratio which will lead to eventual victory, but there will be a price. If you can't accept that then maybe combat sports aren't for you…

- **Evasion** is an effective means of defense. Moving back, out of reach of a kick or takedown attempt, slipping a punch or bobbing under it; there are many possible evasion techniques. Some will take you completely out of the way of an attack, but it is not wise to rely 100% on not getting hit. Often evasion is used to set up a counter, as part of an offensive-defensive technique.
- **Deflection** simply means redirecting an attack. It is often used in conjunction with evasion. Indeed, relying on deflection or evasion alone can be risky, but both together can give you the margin you need. Deflection defenses include batting away punches or kicks (always, always move as well in the case of a kick!).
- **Covering** is a matter of replacing the target with a less critical body part. Often it is passive—punches will frequently strike a good guard or a raised shoulder and thus fail to hit the jaw. While taking any blow is unpleasant, covering will mitigate the effects enough to let you stay in the fight. It must be used intelligently, however. Pathetically covering your head or curling into a ball just prolongs the beating, and MMA fights are stopped when one fighter is no longer intelligently defending himself. Passive covering is not enough. Ideally you should also partially evade the attack and launch a counter of your own.

Defensive moves can be used quite offensively. For example you might "cover up and crash in" to prevent an opponent from striking you. This

Slipping to the outside puts your head well out of a strong-hand blow but still leaves you well positioned to counterattack.

Slipping to the inside can be more risky, but the opponent's next strike can be stopped in its tracks by a quick shot of your own. The slip takes your head out of the way of a punch while allowing you to move in for your own attack.

simply means protecting your head and crashing forwards to get close to the opponent. Once there, you grab him however you can and immobilize his striking weapons. Once the immediate crisis is over you can transition to close-in strikes or set up a takedown.

The Slip

The slip works well against straight punches. Move slightly forward and to the side (you can slip inward or outward depending on circumstances), and cover with your hand, just in case. The opponent's straight punch will go past you, allowing you to come in for an attack of your own.

Bob/Weave

Against a hooked punch, you "bob" down, bending at the legs, and "weave" towards and under the punch. You pass underneath and pop back up outside the opponent's arm ready to counterattack. It is entirely possible to land a good body shot as you pass under the punch. Keep looking forward, not down, and keep your hands up to protect your head in case you don't quite bob down far enough.

Against a hook, Nate (right) crouches and bobs under the strike, letting it pass just over his head.

As the hook goes past, Nate is ready to straighten back up and strike the opponent while he's vulnerable.

Kick Evade

The most basic kick evade is to step backwards, out of reach. This is effective enough but it does not greatly advance your position. Against a straight kick (maybe a push kick or side kick, or the sort of swinging "football kick" that you might encounter on the street), a better option is to step sideways and forward (to the outside or inside; whichever is available at the time) and to scoop the kick away. If you can grab the leg, it is a simple matter to drive forward and topple the opponent even if no more sophisticated takedown is available.

Moving back places you out of reach of a straight kick. If you're quick, you can move forward and strike as the opponent recovers, but often you'll be out of reach and safe but unable to counter. Still, it's a lot better than getting hit!

Moving forward and to the side avoids the kick and places you in range for an attack of your own. This sort of offensive defense is a better route to victory than just scrambling out of reach.

Punch Deflection

Long, straight punches can be patted down or aside with relative ease, which may cause the opponent to go off balance. This sort of defense is usually coupled with a counterpunch.

Pushing an opponent's punch to the side is not just a defensive movement. It can turn his whole body away and open him up to a counterattack.

The Shield

The shield is an effective defense against a roundhouse kick, covering the head, body and leg. You will still have to take the kick, but by moving forward inside the arc of the kick you can weaken it so that it is much less powerful. Your cover protects the areas the kick is designed to damage and lets you stay in the fight. Unless you condition your shins, it may not be a good idea to block shin-to-shin; instead, turn the foot in and use the flesh of your calf to absorb the impact.

The shield is exactly what it says, covering one entire side of your body. Make sure there isn't a big gap between leg and arm, or a kick will come straight through.

Side Head Cover

Covering the head is instinctive, but never hold a fist to your temple unless you're wearing heavy boxing gloves. Your fist will transmit force to your temple as if it was not there at all. Instead, lay your arm along the side of your head and put your hand around the back. If you move forward inside the arc of a blow, you can weaken it and cause it to skid off your cover, round the back of your head. This also brings you in close for a counterattack. It is often a good idea to wrap the opponent's arm with yours, controlling it while you counterattack.

A good cover will mitigate even a heavy blow, to the point where you can ride it and counterattack. Moving forward, inside the arc of a hook punch also helps to weaken it.

Front Cover

The front cover is simply a matter of absorbing impact on your forearms. While unpleasant, this is better than blocking a punch with your face. However, there is a tendency to "fold up" from this position and to want to stay covered up. Do not let that happen; you will need to come out and get back into the fight as soon as possible.

This is only a good way to stop a punch compared to using your head. It's not what you'd choose to do, but sometimes it's the only option. You can't stay here though; at the very least you have to open up the range and collect your wits for a new attack.

Body Cover

Your ribs and flank can be protected by dropping your elbow tight against the body and bracing to meet the impact. If possible, you can flex your body away from the blow to absorb some of its force, but ultimately a body cover will only protect you so much. Get close to the opponent to take as much force as possible out of his strikes.

Body cover can be used as an offensive defense by moving in or sideways to weaken the kick and grabbing the opponent's leg. Just covering and taking the kick is a last resort; you can only take so many of these before you're worn down and unable to fight effectively.

Knee Cover

There are few good options with a knee coming up at you. The best is to put your elbows down and allow the opponent to hit them with his quadriceps. This should discourage him fairly quickly. Failing that, a rising knee can be jammed with forearms or hands (though that is risky). Jamming the knee only stops the attack being made, but if you can grab the leg and hug it against you, the opponent will be controlled and can be taken down fairly easily.

Using your elbows is an offensive defense. If hurts the opponent rather than just defending against his knee strike.

Jamming a knee strike is a viable option, but there's not much to stop the opponent throwing another one, unless you can grab the leg or launch a counterattack.

The Clinch

Even in sports like boxing or kickboxing, where clinching is discouraged, it happens all the time. There are many reasons for initiating a clinch. It can be used to set up a takedown or to protect yourself from an attack. If you get hit hard and need a moment to collect your wits, stumbling backwards is a poor choice as the opponent will simply follow you and keep banging the shots in. It is better to close in and grab him and try to control him while you compose yourself.

Of course, it is also possible to use a clinch to control the opponent while you brutalize him with knees, elbows, and other strikes. This can be harder than it sounds, as you need to get your shots in without losing control over the opponent or being taken down. It takes some practice to become adept

It is instinctive to grab the opponent and pound on him, but trained fighters use the clinch both offensively (to hold and hit the opponent) and defensively (to deny the opponent a chance to land effective strikes) at the same time.

at "dirty boxing" but the results are worth it. The basic principle is to land knees, elbows and hand strikes whenever you can without compromising your balance and position.

There are many, many variations on the clinch. Without splitting hairs about names of techniques, anytime when you grab an opponent and stay close to him, that's a clinch. However, there are several common variations on the theme. In all cases, it is possible to escape from a clinch given enough time. You can make this much harder for the opponent by striking him, pushing and pulling him around, and upsetting his balance.

This section introduces the basic clinch positions. We will be seeing them again, with some techniques that can be performed from these positions, in later sections.

Head Clinches

A two-handed head clinch is often referred to as a "Muay Thai clinch" as it is commonly used in Muay Thai. Both hands go in low around the opponent's neck and meet at the back. Do not interlace your fingers. Keep your elbows down and as close together as possible to prevent him pulling his head out, and drag his head down to your shoulder. Once the opponent is under control you can start delivering knee strikes or set up a takedown.

A one-handed clinch (sometimes called a one-handed collar tie) uses the same principles—one hand is used as a hook around the back of the opponent's neck, with the elbow down. This is not as secure as a two-handed clinch but does allow you to strike the opponent in the ribs or head with

Keep your elbows down and pull the opponent in tight to control him and make escape difficult.

The two-handed clinch is most commonly used to set up knee strikes. Pull the opponent onto the strike as your knee comes up.

your free hand, and to deliver elbow strikes. It is fairly easy to transition from a one-handed clinch to a two-handed one, or to swap hands. The key is to keep the opponent from reacting coherently by striking him and dragging his head around to disorient him.

Nate (right) has established a two-handed head clinch. His opponent struggles to escape, pulling his head back to break away, and loosens Nate's grip...

... Nate allows the opponent to pull away, opening up a gap, and transitions to a single-handed clinch with the other hand...

... creating the opportunity to bang in a short uppercut while pulling the opponent's head onto the strike...

... Nate then violently pulls the opponent's head back onto his shoulder, disorientating him...

... and moves out to the side to deliver a body shot whilst maintaining his complete control of the opponent.

Arm Clinches

When defending a punch it is often instinctive to wrap or "snake" the opponent's striking arm. This is particularly useful against a "street" assailant who may have nothing more than the big swinging right-hand punch in his arsenal. Wrap the arm and tuck it under your armpit, with your forearm behind the opponent's triceps or your hand gripping it. Your other hand can be used to strike with or to grab the opponent around the head for a one-handed collar tie. If you then pull his head onto your shoulder (on the same side as whichever hand is on his head) then you will have good control or a knee strike or while you recover from being hit.

If you can get your forearm behind the opponent's elbow, he will find it hard to pull out. Even if you can't, tightly wrapping the arm will control it while you set up your next move.

This position gives good control of your opponent's movements and can be used to set up a knee strike or takedown attempt.

A clinch does not have to be static. From a head-and-arm clinch, it is possible to transition to an arm wrap, keeping the opponent locked in tight and setting up strikes, then move to a different clinch to keep the opponent on the defensive.

Underhooks

Almost the opposite of an arm clinch, in an underhook you have your arm under the opponent's and around his body. It is common in "vertical grappling" for both fighters to have one underhook and one overhook (i.e. an arm over the opponent's arm). Double-underhooks allow a number of powerful takedowns to be set up, though the position looks weak to those who do not know what to do with it. A single underhook will prevent your opponent from dropping down to launch a double-leg takedown. If he tries, you can simply pull up on his arm.

As with all grappling positions, if you want to make use of underhooks you need to be as close to the opponent as possible. If you can pour water through the gap between you and the opponent, then the gap is too wide. Pull him in close and tight, get him under control, and then do whatever you want to do next.

Even a single underhook makes it impossible to shoot down for a leg takedown. All you have to do is pull upwards and his attempt will fail.

Elementary Takedown Defense

It is possible to end up on the ground for all kinds of reasons, from being knocked down by a blow to simply tripping or losing your balance. Even the best fighter can fall or be deliberately taken down. However, you can do a lot to avoid going to the ground until and unless you want to go there.

It may be obvious, but it is still worth stating that good balance and footwork will greatly improve your chances of keeping your feet. Nor can an opponent take you down if he cannot get a good grip on you. Solid basics are your first line of defense against takedown attempts. Striking from a good posture and withdrawing cleanly afterwards will deny your opponent the chance to grab your arm or leg for a takedown. The effects of a good strike or kick will often stop any attempt at countering with a grab or takedown.

If this fails and the opponent does manage to get hold of you, then your best option is to "base out" and try to deny him a good grip. Basing out

I've (left) checked the inside of Gary's arm, blocking his grab attempt. From here I could snake over and wrap his arm, or drive underneath it for an underhook, or I could hook my left arm inward and take a one-handed head clinch...or just punch him in the face.

I've deflected Gary's grab attempt to my right, placing me "outside" his arm and breaking his posture. This is a very common control-and-restraint position, but striking is also an option from here.

simply means dropping your center of gravity as much as possible and widening your stance. Fighting for grips is an essential part of wrestling and judo training, and there is no substitute for hours of experience. However, even just messing about with a bit of fun wrestling is beneficial.

A good clinch position (see above) will prevent the opponent from attempting a takedown, and this is one of the reasons for clinching the opponent. It is, of course, not enough to simply resist a takedown attempt. It's safe to assume that if you end up grappling with someone for any length of time, the fight will go to the ground whether you want it to or not.

The reason a lot of "street" fights end up on the ground is an inability to effectively deal with a grab. What often happens is that one fighter grabs the other and both end up lurching around until someone falls, sometimes dragging the opponent down with him. Usually this is not a deliberate attempt at a takedown but the inevitable consequence of close-quarters wrestling.

Thus, it is necessary to deal actively with a takedown attempt, rather than to simply resist and hope for the best. Your counter may be a takedown of your own, or perhaps a striking solution may be a better option.

While there are many possible takedowns and throws that might be attempted, most depend upon establishing an advantageous clinch position and can be countered by good clinch skills on your part. Of the takedowns that are launched from beyond clinch range, most attack the legs. A

Gary (right) shoots in for a double-leg takedown. Even untrained fighters will try something like this from time to time, though it will not be very well executed. I haven't reacted in time, so even a poor attempt has a good chance of dumping me on my back.

single-leg takedown will normally be launched against your lead leg while a double-leg takedown, as the name suggests, attempts to use both legs. The sort of waist tackle that often occurs in a street fight is essentially a poor version of the double-leg takedown.

Any leg takedown is dangerous, as it can put you down so hard that you are pretty much out of the fight. Thus any defense you make must be correctly judged; you cannot afford to fail here. On the other hand, leg takedowns are very committed and do offer some good opportunities to a successful defender. For example, it is possible to bring up a knee at the right moment and allow the opponent to smash himself into it, face first. If successful this can be a fight-ender but it is risky as it could leave you on one foot as the takedown arrives.

Alternative defenses are to dump, jam, or sprawl.

Dump Defense

As the opponent comes in low, with his head down, you move back a little and deflect him downwards by dropping your hands hard onto the back of his neck as if you were looking for a Thai clinch. Essentially you bash his head downwards, and since he is already committed to shooting in, he will continue downward and crash into the ground where your feet were before you moved. Something similar happens if he misjudges the distance or you step back at just the right moment; he may project himself to the ground in front of you.

The most elementary defense against a takedown of this sort is distance. I've suddenly moved backwards, and the takedown attempt is now heading for empty air. If I'm lucky he'll dive into the floor at my feet...

... but this time I've dropped my hands onto the back of his neck as I move out of reach, slamming him face-first into the mats.

Jam Defense

As the opponent shoots in, jam his movement by placing your hands on his shoulders and pushing him away from you. He should turn to one side, allowing you to follow up with knees or other strikes.

Gary shoots in for a takedown, catching me by surprise. It's too late to try to move out of range...

... my best option is to drop my weight onto Gary's back and drive my front hip forward...

... and move my back leg right back, where he can't get a good grip on it.

If Gary tries to pick up my front leg for a single-leg takedown, my weight is on it and my center of gravity is low. I'm safe enough unless he can drive me backwards and shorten my stance.

It is also (sometimes) possible to defeat a leg takedown by pushing your lead-side hip forward and placing a lot of weight on your lead leg, preventing it from being picked up while your rear leg is well behind and out of reach. This can leave you with an opponent hanging from your waist, which is not always a good thing. It does set you up well to apply a guillotine choke, however.

The traditional "elbow to spine" can also be delivered at this point, but it is not actually all that effective. It is better to drop elbows or hammerfists in under the opponent's shoulder blades to empty his lungs. It may also be possible to force him to the ground by pushing him down. If instead he breaks away, you can follow up as above.

Sprawl Defense

As the opponent shoots in for his takedown attempt, move both your feet well back so that you start to fall forwards. Your weight lands on the opponent's back and drives him to the ground. If he tries to stay up, grip him firmly around the floating ribs with your arms and shake him violently. This should bring him down.

As Gary (left) shoots in, I skip my feet as far back as I can get them, dropping my weight onto his back. Sprawling like this guarantees that I'm still going to the ground, but I'm going on my terms, not his.

I land on Gary's back and keep my weight on him. Now we start fighting for a dominant position, and I'm starting out with a huge advantage.

The disadvantage of the sprawl is that it takes you to the ground, which may not be what you want. However, it is the most reliable defense against a well-executed double-leg takedown. If the opponent's attack is launched from too far out or is hesitant or poorly executed, then jamming it and staying on your feet is a good idea. However, if it looks like a good one, it is best not to take the risk. In this case, choose the sprawl as the consequences of a failed defense are—at the very least—going to the ground hard in a highly disadvantageous position.

Building a Toolkit

It is, as a rule, far better to have a few general-purpose techniques in your arsenal—and to be good at using them—than a lot of clever variations that you will struggle to apply. Most effective fighters have a "main toolkit" which gives them something they can use in most situations, plus a larger collection of more specialized techniques that they might use if the right circumstances present themselves.

A basic set of strikes, a couple of takedowns and a few submissions are really all you need. It is good to know more, especially as a wider body of technique can give you options that might not otherwise be available. However, it is far more important to be able to do a few things well than a lot of things adequately. Against a trained opponent, adequate will often not be enough.

This is where many martial artists go astray. Endlessly drilling the same fairly simple movements is boring, and many martial artists want to judge their ability on how many techniques they know or how impressive their skills. Fact is, it's not how much you know that counts, it's what you can do under fight conditions.

Most fighters use a fairly limited selection of techniques nearly all the time, with more complex or impressive material coming out quite rarely. Thus it makes sense to develop a limited set of techniques to a very high level, and to pay attention to the little things that make them work. You can add extra techniques when you have a solid foundation.

Many students want to learn exciting techniques like high kicks. It's one thing to do this on a pad or heavy bag, but something else entirely to make it work in the middle of a fight.

A simple rule of thumb is that a fighter who can do a few basic things well, at the right time, and with confidence, will defeat a martial artist who has spread his training time thinly among a vast array of techniques. The latter is a wide but shallow puddle, while the former is a narrow but deep crack full of dark water waiting to engulf you.

We have chosen a basic "toolkit" of twenty techniques that will give you a reasonable set of options. There is nothing complex or flashy in here, nor anything that will take more than a few minutes to learn. However, mastering these techniques so that they can be delivered effectively and reliably while someone is punching you in the face will take a bit longer.

The techniques we have chosen do not cover all possible eventualities but they will give you an effective all-round fighting system which can be used to win a fight standing up or on the ground. Extras can be added as your skill increases, but it is always worth spending time on the basics.

It is worth paying serious attention to the principles that make any given technique work. Not only is this one of the hidden "secrets" of the

Drilling is essentially (but not excessively) cooperative. Once the technique has been properly learned then the time will come to test it against resistance. For now, the fighters work together to improve one another's skills.

Keith (on top) uses both hands to control one of his opponent's arms, allowing him to establish the position he wants. Chris does not make it too easy for him, but nor does he try to mess up Keith's technique.

Once he has his opponent's arm positioned and under control, Keith can release one hand to make his next move. Chris gives feedback on whether his arm is properly controlled and whether the technique would work "for real."

Since this is a drill, Chris does not resist too much as Keith (on top) brings his hands together, but he does not let Keith succeed unless he is applying the technique correctly. In competitive rolling, Chris would do whatever he could to prevent Keith from establishing this position; here, he might actually talk Chris through the technique if something is not right.

Having proceeded through all the stages of the technique, Keith applies the lock and Chris taps to let him know it's worked properly. Both fighters communicate truthfully during the drill, whereas in competition they would try to deceive one another.

effective fighter but it will also give you a good foundation upon which to add extra techniques.

Many would-be fighters neglect the underlying principles behind their techniques. For example, it is not uncommon to see someone mindlessly banging away at the heavy bag. This is fine for fitness but if the goal is improving technique then it is possible to get more out of the time spent on it. Working on positioning, weight transference, and a clean return to guard makes these things into habits, which in turn means you are more likely to do them when you're under pressure.

The Twenty Techniques

The following chapters present a basic toolkit of just 20 techniques, which cover a wide range of possible circumstances. You may decide to add a couple more or to swap in an alternative here and there, but learning to perform this repertoire of strikes, kicks, takedowns, and submissions will give you a good set of options that will cover most eventualities.

- Lead Hand Strike
- Cross/Rear Hand Strike
- Hook/Hammerfist
- Body Shot/Shovel Hook
- Uppercut

- Elbow Strike
- Knee Strike
- Push Kick
- Roundhouse Kick
- Outer/Inner Reaping Takedown

- Single Leg Takedown
- Double Leg Takedown
- Outer Wheel Takedown
- Front or Side Body Lock Takedown
- Clinch Takedown
- Bar Choke/Rear Naked Choke
- Triangle Choke
- Guillotine Choke
- Straight Arm Lock (Arm Bar)
- Shoulder Lock (Kimura and Americana)

It may seem obvious to suggest that techniques should be drilled intelligently and with due regard to their underlying principles, but many fighters become complacent and simply bash away instead, or spend all their time working on submissions without drilling the set-ups and positional skills that make them work. The flaws in this approach are not always apparent in a class. Some martial artists manage to look awesome in the class with their complex techniques and subtle variations, but the real test is a fight, and it is there that you will find out whether you can make a technique work despite your opponent's resistance… or whether you can merely perform it in class.

Once you have established a good, all-around toolkit, and you can do all of your chosen techniques well, then you may want to start adding to it. Exactly what you choose to add is a matter of personal preference and judgment in terms of usefulness. You might want to add a flashy submission simply because you like it and it impresses the crowds. If so, that's fine as long as you're realistic about how often it will be useful. Obsessing about trying to pull off a "Submission of the Night" with your favorite move can make you pass up less impressive opportunities to finish the fight.

On the other hand, your added techniques might be more workaday material. There are many obvious choices that are not listed in our suggested toolkit above. Side kicks, leg submissions, and additional takedowns are all strong candidates for inclusion. Alternatively, if you train in a specific martial art, then the techniques of that art are obvious candidates for inclusion.

It is best to add new material one technique at a time, and work it up to the point where you can use it effectively before you add something else. Exploring variations and applications of existing techniques is also a good option. For example, something as simple as an arm bar can be applied from many positions. It is more advisable to learn to use a given technique for many applications and in many situations than to add something entirely different to your arsenal.

CHAPTER 4

Groundfighting Basics

Basic Principles

Much of the time, a fight that has gone to the ground looks like an unholy mess. However, even when untrained people are scrapping on the ground there are certain positions that emerge where one gains the advantage. These are not stylized positions invented by martial artists to fill out a grading syllabus; they are the result of observation of what actually happens in a groundfight.

As a general rule, it is necessary to establish a good position before trying to finish the fight. This is the groundfighter's mantra: "Position Before Submission" and it applies equally to attempts to ground and pound your opponent. It is possible to obtain a submission hold or to land good strikes from almost anywhere, but the odds are much, much better if you first establish a good solid position.

Ideally, you want to obtain a dominant position where you have weight on your opponent and you can wear him down simply through the increased

Order will emerge from all this chaos... sooner or later. We're both trying to hook limbs or head and get the opponent under control as we work towards a dominant position. Eventually one of us will achieve a recognizable position.

As soon as your opponent hits the ground, your first task is to get him under control. Grab and control any limb you can, or the head, to limit the opponent's options. Once a measure of control is established, you can begin working towards a dominant position.

effort of breathing. If you achieve a dominant position in a refereed fight, it is possible to "lay and pray," waiting for the end of the round in the hope that the judges will decide in your favor. This isn't the best way to win a match but it generally works.

"Lay and pray" is not a good idea on the street. Your goal should be to get back to your feet as quickly as possible. This does not preclude doing some damage before you get up of course, but rolling around in the street looking for an arm bar is not usually a good strategy.

There are those that think that MMA groundfighting skills are all-conquering on the street, and those that say they are invalid because the opponent might bite or poke your eyes. The truth is somewhere in between; groundfighting (and indeed all fighting) is about using the tools you have to the best advantage, and positional skills are all about putting you where you can use your tools and the opponent will struggle to use his.

Armbars, guillotine chokes, bites, and eye gouges are all just tools. Both you and the opponent have more options on the street where there are no rules, but the skills that will make those options work and deny them to the opponent are equally applicable to the street and the sporting venue.

Positional skills are of paramount importance on the ground; more so perhaps than the submission techniques themselves. Many people fixate on training their submissions, but without the skills to put yourself where the submission can work, they are virtually worthless. Similarly, if your standup game is pathetic you may never get a chance to apply your excellent submission skills—you'll be knocked out or taken down in a hugely disadvantageous position and stand no chance of getting back into the fight.

Establishing a good, solid dominant position allows you to consider your options and select which submission or striking technique is most appropriate. It also ensures that the technique you choose has an excellent chance of success.

A basic defensive tactic is to get your knee into the gap between you and the opponent. If you can prevent him from getting his center of gravity down low, you may be able to roll him off or over using your leg.

Keeping weight on the opponent is vital to the success of any submission attempt or maintaining a dominant position. Weight on the hips prevents any attempt to turn, and pushing down on the chest counters an attempt to grab and pull you down.

Poorly trained fighters are often so keen to look for a submission or start dropping punches on your head that they compromise their position. A weak position like this does not control the opponent and is just begging to be reversed.

So, whether you're in a sporting bout or a barfight, the same principles apply. If you're in a disadvantaged position you have to get out of it. If you can achieve a dominant position you can then do what you want: get up and escape, or apply a finishing move. It can be tempting to try to rush into a submission or escape attempt, but that usually just wastes energy without achieving anything useful. Instead, you must work methodically. Obtain a position, establish it, then make your attempt.

The key to minimizing damage from strikes or the opponent's chances of a successful submission, or to making your own techniques work, is to get him under control. If you are on the top then your weight is an asset here. You must keep weight on the opponent all the time, whatever else you are doing. If not, then he will escape.

At the same time, you need to avoid being reversed and letting your opponent achieve a dominant position. The key to this is your ability to base out. This is pretty instinctive; if you are being tipped over to the right, you will instinctively use your right arm or leg to support you, reaching out wide to create a stable support. Keeping your weight low also helps prevent reversal. It is necessary to "posture up" in order to drop blows on an opponent, but you need to maintain a solid base while you do it, or you'll be reversed.

If you are on the bottom, you need to control your opponent to prevent him striking downwards at you. It is possible to strike effectively upwards but the advantage is always with the fighter on the top in an exchange of blows. Even children and drunks know this; in fights outside bars or in the schoolyard you will see attempts to get on top and start dropping bombs

Strange as it might look, it is well worth practicing the "shrimp" movement. Note where Nate's center of gravity is right now.

Bring up a leg to push with and begin to fold up using your abdominal muscles to pull you rapidly into a "shrimp" position. The aim is to scoot, butt-first, out from under what is pinning you down.

Push hard with your foot and curl into the "shrimp" position. Note how far Nate's center of gravity has moved. A partial shrimp can also used to set up submissions.

The bridge and roll is another staple groundfighting technique. It can be used to dislodge an opponent's dominant position or roll him right off you.

Explosively drive your hips upward and roll to whichever side you choose.

The aim is to turn right over and escape from a bad position, but even a failed bridge will weaken the opponent's position and make him concentrate on basing out rather than smashing you in the head or setting up a submission.

Patience is often the key to success in grappling. With the opponent under control, you can get a few breaths in while you wait for the right moment to act. With luck, he might become impatient and make a mistake that you can exploit.

on the opponent. Upwards strikes are useful but they are a distraction, not a tool for winning fights. Don't expect great things when trying to punch upwards from your back.

Controlling an opponent who is on top of you uses many of the same principles as the clinch. You can trap an arm or pull the opponent down by his head. This will not win the fight but it minimizes the damage he can do to you while you work on an escape. If you are going to try to turn the opponent and get out from under him, you need to prevent him from basing. That means trapping the arm and leg on that side before attempting the turn, or it will fail.

Good groundfighters develop "tactile sensitivity," which means that they can feel what the opponent is trying to do. They also learn to relax as much as possible and conserve energy. Where an inexperienced fighter will constantly exert himself and may soon become exhausted, a more seasoned competitor waits for the right moment and then acts explosively.

It is a good idea to keep your opponent under pressure to prevent him from thinking carefully about how to escape, but do not exhaust yourself. You must do something though, even if you are essentially taking a rest. If you do not, the referee will separate you to prevent the fight from becoming too boring.

The Guard

There are numerous variations on the concept of the guard, but the principles are the same. The fighter uses his legs to control the opponent and prevent him from doing whatever he wants. Although there are many possible submissions from the guard, it is essentially a defensive position, as the name suggests. If the fight goes to a decision you are unlikely to be given the victory if you spent lengthy periods on your back, even if you made creditable efforts at obtaining a submission.

A closed guard will keep the opponent under good control, but it will not prevent strikes. His strikes will be weakened, however, and if you can control one or both of his arms then his options are severely limited.

An open guard does not control the dominant opponent as well as a closed guard, but it offers more possibilities to reverse or escape from the situation.

Nate (on the bottom) establishes a closed guard to stop Gary from moving into a stronger position and tries to grab his arms to prevent any strikes coming in…

… Gary yanks his arm free to strike Nate. Nate lunges up and grabs Gary around the head…

… and pulls Gary in tight. Gary can still deliver some strikes but his options are limited and Nate's arms and shoulders provide some protection for his head and body. With his opponent under control, Nate can begin working to improve the situation.

Thus it is best to view the guard as a position used to avoid defeat, and to work on getting into a better position or back to your feet. The two main variants on the guard are open and closed. A fighter using a closed guard prevents the opponent from moving by locking his ankles together behind the opponent's back, creating a tight grip. An open guard is, as the name suggests, open at the rear with the fighter's feet usually planted on the ground. It may be possible to hook ("grapevine") one or both of the opponent's feet with your own, breaking his posture and weakening his base.

The dominant fighter may try to control his opponent by pushing down on hips, chest, or biceps, and may drop hammerfists or punches on his opponent. This is less effective from guard than mount, and it does allow the opponent to try to grab and wrap the striking arm or pull the dominant fighter down with what is essentially a head clinch. This limits what the dominant fighter can do, but he can still deliver hooked strikes to the body and head.

Half-Guard

This variation on the basic guard position occurs very frequently. The dominant fighter has one leg free but the other is between the opponent's legs. The opponent wraps his legs around the leg he can control and uses this to prevent the dominant fighter from achieving a better position such as side control or the mount. In general, the dominant fighter will try to get his leg free and the opponent will try to obtain a full guard position.

This is what half-guard is for. Nate has partially got out of my guard and is moving into side control, but if I cross my ankles over his leg I can stop him getting any further.

Reversal from the Guard

The most basic reversal from the guard position attempts to roll the opponent over and end up in a mount position. It can only be done from an open guard. It is necessary to control the arm on the side that the dominant fighter is to be rolled towards, to prevent him from basing out.

Nate (on the bottom) establishes a closed guard and immobilizes one of Gary's hands against his chest. This deprives Gary of the support of this hand if Nate rolls him in this direction.

Keeping Gary's striking hand under control as best he can, Nate opens up his guard. Hopefully Gary will be so focused on launching a punch that he doesn't immediately realize what is happening…

… as Nate grabs Gary's trapped hand with both of his and rolls him in that direction. At the same time, Nate pushes Gary's body with his leg. If the reversal is successful, the punch will not land if not, well, that's a risk that has to be taken.

Nate has trapped Gary's left hand and his leg is outside Gary's left leg, preventing him from using either to widen his base. Gary is unable to prevent himself from being rolled over…

… allowing Nate to establish a mount position, which he immediately secures by widening his own base and dropping his weight on Gary. Once the position is well locked in, Nate will begin to exploit it.

The defending fighter traps one of the opponent's arms by holding it to his chest or wrapping it with an arm and holding it against his ribs. He prevents the opponent from basing out with his leg by using his own leg on that side to either "grapevine" around the opponent's leg or simply push against it. The defending fighter forces his opposite leg under the opponent's body and uses it to push him up and over, rolling him towards the trapped hand. This movement needs to be explosive and momentum must be maintained to roll right over and land on top.

Alternatively, it may be possible to knock out the opponent's supporting leg while tipping him over to that side. The defending fighter wraps his opponent's arm and places his foot on the same side on the opponent's thigh or hip. He makes room for this movement by shrimping; rolling slightly onto his side and pushing his lower back out.

The defending fighter then pushes the opponent's opposite shoulder up with the arm that is not trapping that of the opponent, and drives the foot on that side down hard onto the ground, attempting to roll himself and the opponent over. At the same time he straightens his other leg, pushing the supporting leg out from under his opponent. This is one explosive movement which will hopefully result in a reversal i.e. the previously dominant fighter will find himself on the bottom, with his opponent in a mount position.

A failed sweep can still be useful. It may make enough of a gap (by pushing the dominant fighter away) to allow the defender to scoot free and get back to his feet.

Guard Pass

Sometimes, the best option when in an opponent's guard is to back out and let him stand up, especially if you are a good striker and the opponent is a strong groundfighter. If you do want to advance your position on the ground, you need to get out of the opponent's guard and into a better position. This means passing the guard somehow. There are various options. We will consider just two; going around it or climbing over it.

First, it is necessary to break a closed guard if the opponent has one. Push one knee as far under his buttocks as you can to obtain leverage, and push his legs down and apart using your elbows against his inner thighs. This is painful, but pain alone will not always break a determined fighter's guard; this is where the extra leverage is useful.

With the guard broken you may be able to push a leg down and hold it there by moving your knee past the leg before putting your weight back down. This holds the door open, so to speak, by keeping the opponent's leg down. From there it is possible to bring the other leg through and move into a mount position.

Chris (on the bottom) is using a closed guard to limit Keith's options.

Keith needs to break the guard, which he does by digging his elbow into the inner thigh and pushing down.

With the guard now broken, Keith pushes the leg down.

Keith pins the leg with his own and starts to climb over and round.

Keith hooks his left foot over the opponent's leg to keep it controlled. If he neglected to do this, Chris could snap a half-guard closed on his leg and prevent further movement.

Still keeping his opponent's leg trapped, Keith continues round...

... and into side control, keeping weight on his opponent's chest the whole time.

Alternatively, you can go around the guard by scooping one leg up using the crook of your arm behind the knee. Lift it up and over your head, and quickly duck under to get out to the side. Slam the leg down again and keep as much weight on it as you can while you move around into a side control position.

I've succeeded in breaking Nate's closed guard.

I force my arm under his leg, scooping it up high...

... and throw it over my head. As the same time I scoot around and drop my weight onto Nate to prevent him re-establishing a defensive position.

Sometimes the opponent turns right over, sometimes he doesn't. Either way, get your weight on him, establishing a solid side control position, before you try to do anything else.

Side Control

Side control is arguably the best of the dominant positions as it gives you many options and is hard to reverse. You want to be chest to chest with the opponent, making an "L" or "T" shape, with your weight on his chest. Many fighters push their hand under the opponent's head to anchor the position while others leave it free. Both are good options, but what is certain is that you need to keep your hips as close to the floor as possible to avoid being reversed.

The side control position is hard to dislodge and offers many options for submissions.

It is also possible to suddenly pop up and drop a big shot into your opponent's head, then drop down again and re-establish your control. Taking your weight off the opponent is always a risk, but if it is well timed and done quickly he may not have time to react.

Alternatively, you can drive knees into the opponent's head or body. This requires some lifting of your weight, so it should be done suddenly and fast. Don't try to stay up and keep slamming in knees or the opponent will escape; instead re-establish your position between strikes.

Pulling elbows into the opponent's head and body is a good option that does not disturb your position much. These strikes are not fight-enders but they will wear down an opponent.

There are many options from side control. You can always pull elbow strikes into the head and body, and slam knee strikes in from the other side. It is possible to pulverize an opponent from here, and difficult to escape. One way to do so is for the defending fighter to get his arms between himself and his opponent, and to try to lift the dominant fighter over his head while scooting out from underneath in the direction his feet are pointing or shrimping to the side away from the opponent.

Alternatively, it may be possible to force the knee nearest the dominant fighter underneath him and drive it through, obtaining a guard position, or to shrimp out from underneath and stand up.

Nate has established side control. I first prevent things from getting any worse by grabbing him anyway I can.

I force my arm over his head, rolling my shoulder forward to add force and make some space for what I want to do next. I also bring up my left foot, ready to push.

I jam my other arm elbow-first under his hip, getting it in as deep as I can. This position gives me some control and protection from strikes, but I have no intention of staying here.

I push up with my left arm and push down on my opponent's head, sitting up as I do so. I keep the momentum going by pushing with my left foot

I roll into side control, gripping Nate's arm to prevent him repeating what I just did.

I have side control. Nate pushes his arms under my body. This makes him vulnerable to strikes while his hands are trapped, but not for long…

He explosively bridges and hurls me off, over his head. By the time I've recovered he can be on his feet or moving into establish a dominant position of his own.

North-South

The north-south position is one that many fighters find it difficult to use effectively, and so tends to be used as a "rest" rather than an attempt to set up a submission. It can occur accidentally or while one fighter is trying to transition to a more advantageous position. The fighter on the bottom is, technically speaking, "losing" while held in north-south but it is extremely unlikely that the referee would allow the opponent to simply stay there for the rest of the round. More likely, he will use north-south to get a few breaths in and to obtain control, and then transition to a better position to seek a finish.

The north-south position is not a particularly pleasant place to be, but there is a lim-it to what the dominant fighter can achieve from here. Most commonly it is a posi-tion that is passed through on the way to something better, rather than somewhere a fighter wants to be.

It is sometimes possible to reverse north-south by simply rolling over, though this requires good timing to catch the opponent unawares and unable to base out in time. A sudden, explosive roll driven by the opposite foot, tightly holding the opponent and turning him, can work. It is also sometimes possible to break the opponent's grip by shrimping to the side and twisting free.

The Mount

The mount is an instinctive dominant position, holding down the opponent by kneeling astride him. Some fighters will try to hold the opponent down by kneeling on one or both arms. The mount is a great position for rain-ing down strikes but it is important not to become overly enthusiastic; a fighter who raises his center of gravity can easily be reversed. Numerous submissions can also be performed from the mount.

The opponent can be temporarily prevented from doing serious damage by clinching him and pulling him down. Normally this means grabbing the back of his head as if applying a Thai clinch, but it is also possible to wrap an arm or grab around the body with what amounts to a double underhook. This is not a long-term solution but it can be used to protect yourself while you find a way to escape.

Escaping from the mount can be very easy if the opponent is careless and does not establish a solid position. The typical "street fight" mount is simple enough to dislodge as the attacker is usually too busy punching to base out. If the opponent's center of gravity is high, it is possible to "bump" him off by either bucking the hips upwards or kneeing him in the buttocks and pulling him over your head. This also works against a trained man if he has not properly established his position, but once a trained fighter has firmly established his mount position your chances are poor.

Even untrained fighters will instinctively try to get on top and rain down blows. Most are so intent on hitting that they forget about their position and are easy to dislodge.

Against a trained fighter, you typically get just one chance to bump him off, as he first establishes his position. He might give you another chance if he gets a bit over-enthusiastic with his ground-and-pound. First, you have to protect yourself from his strikes...

... then bump him forward with your knee or by bridging explosively. Pull him forward at the same time...

... and roll on top as he goes to one side or the other.

You will almost certainly end up in his guard, but that is a significant improvement on being under a well locked-in mount.

A mount can be reversed by rolling to the side. You will need to trap an arm and the leg on the same side. If the opponent it striking from the mount then a cover-and-wrap movement will get you the arm. You will need to grapevine the foot on that side and pull it in tight towards the opponent's centerline. Push down hard with your foot on the opposite side and push up with the hand on that side, rolling the opponent over. You will land on top of him, in his guard. This is not the best place in the world to be, but it is an improvement.

To reverse a mount you have to trap an arm. That requires good timing, and you'll receive some strikes until you succeed.

Get over the top of the opponent's arm and snake around it...

... wrapping it tightly. Pull the arm close to your body. Whichever arm you trap, that's the direction in which you'll roll the opponent.

Push hard with the opposite foot or bridge violently, rolling towards the trapped arm. The opponent cannot use it to base out and will be rolled off you. Chances are you'll end up in his guard, so be ready to work on a guard pass.

Knee Ride

A knee ride, or knee-on position, is extremely unpleasant. The dominant fighter puts his weight on whichever knee is on the opponent's stomach and bears down. This is an effective position for ground-and-pound and can severely limit breathing. The "knee drop" is effective on the street. Rather than place a knee on the defender's body, the dominant fighter drops his weight behind the knee for an extremely destructive strike. This is not allowed in most competitions.

Nate has plenty of options from this position. The simplest option would be to allow his right knee to buckle and drop with his weight behind it onto Rick's ribs. This is illegal in many competitions for reasons of fighter safety, but it can be highly effective as a "street" finish.

A knee ride can be used to hold down and control an opponent while you strike him or set up a finishing move. If you drop the knee in hard with your weight behind it, you may well break some of the opponent's ribs, so for competition and training purposes the knee is placed rather than dropped.

If you pull up on the opponent's head and leg, he will be unable to escape and will struggle to breathe. This can soften him up or even force a submission.

Shrimping is again the best defense, ideally accompanied by batting the opponent's knee to the side. This is best done before the position is properly established. If the dominant fighter is not careful to establish a solid position, he can be dislodged relatively easily, but once the knee is sunk into the defender's body it becomes difficult to push it aside. At the same time, the defender may be unable to reach up high enough to topple the dominant fighter off him.

As the opponent attempts to settle his knee on you, push it away and turn to the side...

... shrimping out from under the threat. This may not work once the knee ride is firmly anchored in position, so act early and decisively.

CHAPTER 5
Straight Strikes

General Principles

Straight strikes, as the name suggests, travel directly from wherever your hands happen to be, to the target. Most commonly, this is the head. Downward body strikes are ineffective due to the construction of the body, which effectively protects its internal organs from downward impact. An upward or horizontal strike is much more effective against the body.

There are various ways to deliver a straight strike, each with their own applications. In a sporting context, a closed fist protected by gloves (be they MMA or boxing gloves) is most common. However, even with gloves and hand wraps there is always the danger of breaking the small bones of the hand or injuring the wrist. A good tight fist will help, but the risk is never entirely eliminated.

A good substitute for a closed fist is a palm strike. This is used in many military combative systems and self-defense styles. The hand is pulled back out of the way, using the fleshy base of the palm as a striking surface. This protects the hand from damage and delivers good impact. There is no need to worry about exactly how to form the hand or hold the fingers, so long as they are kept clear of the impact. An open hand can be used to "smash and grab"(striking then grabbing the opponent's flesh or clothing).

If striking with unprotected hands, a good rule is "hard weapon to soft target, soft weapon to hard target." This means that fists are best employed for body shots where they will not strike bone, and palms work well against bony targets such as the jaw or skull. The comments in this chapter apply equally to a palm shot or a blow with the fist.

The same mechanics are used for a punch or a palm strike. Only the striking surface changes.

A closed fist is standard for striking. With gloves, the risk of damage to the hand when hitting something hard like bone is greatly reduced.

A palm strike uses the heel of the hand instead of the knuckles, and does not risk hand damage. Simply, it's just a punch with the hand pulled back.

Lead Hand Strike

Most people, even many trained fighters, cannot strike effectively with the lead hand. A good lead hand can be used to keep an opponent at a distance or set up more powerful strikes. It can also interrupt what the opponent is doing or distract him, drawing his guard away from where you want to attack. A good enough lead hand can put an opponent on his back, but few fighters spend the time required to develop the skill required for this. All the same, lead hand strikes are an essential part of your repertoire.

Throw a lead hand shot from your guard position without drawing your hand back. It should travel straight to the target with no hooking.

Keep the back hand up to defend, and ready to follow with a cross.

Move into range and launch the strike without any retraction or chambering...

... extending straight out to the opponent's eyes. This strike is primarily for self-defense but can be used as a training tool, teaching students not to draw their hand back before throwing a lead hand shot.

A lead hand strike should be fast, but still hit as hard as possible. Some fighters use the lead hand "jab" as little more than a distraction and range-finding tool, but if you are going to use energy to throw a shot, you might as well get your money's worth. As already noted, a lead hand shot will not drop an opponent but it will wear him down.

A lead shot is thrown from your guard, with no retraction. It travels in a straight line, i.e. it is not in any way hooked. As with all strikes, breathe out as the strike is thrown but stay relaxed until the moment of impact. Tense up your body to drive the strike into the opponent, then relax and snap back to guard. Do not allow the spent strike to drop after impact or you will be wide open. Your lead shoulder should be hunched slightly (not too much though) to protect your jaw, but you want that hand back in place as soon as possible.

The lead hand can also be used for an eye strike. This is entirely illegal in competition but can be useful in a self-defense context. An eye strike can be a back-of-the-hand flick or a stabbing motion at the eyes. It is not really possible to destroy eyeballs this way, but an opponent may be temporarily blinded. He will certainly flinch, allowing you to launch a follow-up strike. An eye jab/palm strike combination is a good option for self-defense and uses the same principles as the conventional jab-cross used by boxers.

The Cross

Straight shots with the rear (power) hand are the staple of most striking systems, and rightly so. A good straight shot is a fight-ender on the street

A cross usually follows a successful lead-hand shot, but can be thrown on its own. Either way, it comes from guard position with no big wind-up or chambering.

The cross comes from the back foot and is pushed into the target with body weight behind it. Afterwards, get back to your guard ready to follow up or deal with the opponent's response.

or in competition, but it needs to be properly set up to get the best possible result. The usual setup for trained fighters is a lead hand punch; "street" opponents will often grab with the lead hand and try to pull you onto the cross instead.

A good cross is thrown from your guard with no retraction and no hooking. Do not hit "to" the target, hit "through" it. That is to say, your intended impact point should be inside the opponent's head or body rather than on the surface. As with all strikes, the more force you dump into the target, the better, but it is also important to deliver force quickly. A hard but slow cross is essentially a push. It will push the opponent away rather than causing brain shake or impact damage.

You can best see this on the heavy bag; a shot that makes the bag swing about is "pushy," while one that dents it and makes it shudder is more likely to put an opponent down. In all cases, strikes are not thrown with just the arms. A cross comes from the back foot and is driven into the target by pushing the hip and shoulder forward as well as the arm.

Using Straight Strikes

The lead and cross are your bread-and-butter striking techniques and should be drilled constantly. They are used to keep the opponent from being able to do what he wants, to control distance, and of course to wear him down over the course of the fight. Often, it is not the lead or cross

Rick tags Nate with a fast lead-hand strike, opening him up for the big cross.

Nate might fall, or stumble in an unexpected direction, or do something entirely unpredictable, so Rick needs to evaluate where best to put his next attack. The instant he takes to do this is time well spent if it ensures the next shot is a fight-ender.

that gets a result, but what follows them. However, a good set of straight strikes can buy you the opportunity you need for a finishing move.

After hitting (with fist or palm, as noted above), it is vital to snap quickly back to guard and launch something else. It only takes an instant to see what the opponent is doing, and it is necessary to do so. The only reason he will be exactly where he was when you launched your strike is if you did not hit him hard enough (or at all). A good strike will move the opponent or make him flinch; it is both embarrassing and potentially costly for your follow-up to fail because your strikes pushed the opponent out of reach or made him flinch in a way that spoiled your technique.

So take an instant to evaluate what the opponent is doing and establish a good solid base to throw from before your next attack. Your strikes will buy you the time to do this.

Many fighters endlessly drill lead/cross combinations that are essentially a single technique made up of two strikes. This is an excellent combination, but it can make you predictable—everyone expects a lead hand shot to be followed by a cross. So it is worth drilling other follow-ups. You can set an opponent up by using repeated lead shots before putting in the big cross, or doing something entirely different like throwing a lead then shooting in for a takedown as he moves to cover the cross he is expecting.

There is also a tendency to neglect the early parts of a combination while rushing to the big finish. This applies to all manner of techniques, not just a one-two lead/cross combination. Everyone wants to get to the submission or the big knockout blow, but getting there requires taking all the steps along the way. If your opening move (in this case the lead hand shot) is poor because you did not perform it properly, it may not set the opponent up for the finish (in this case the cross). The big finish has to be earned, and the way you earn it is to put the proper effort into each step along the way.

Striking upward is a good cardio drill, which also has benefits for punching technique even if you never find yourself striking from under the mount.

It is critical to get as much of your body into the strike as you can, rolling your shoulders into the shot...

... and powering the strike by pushing on the ground with your legs.

Gravity is not your friend here, but you can still learn to deliver some potent strikes that may prevent an opponent from establishing a good mount position and submitting or ground-and-pounding you.

CHAPTER 6

Hooked Strikes

General Principles

Hooking shots are the most instinctive of punches, and perhaps for this reason many fighters execute them badly. A well-placed hook with the lead or power hand will drop many opponents and can be used to get around a tight guard.

As with straight strikes, the striking surface does not have to be the knuckles of the hand. The base of a tight fist can be used (i.e. a hammerfist). Hammerfists are an excellent variation on the hook theme and can be used in circumstances where it is not possible to punch effectively. For example, a hammerfist can be dropped into an opponent's thigh muscles during a clinch.

A hooked shot does not need an obvious wind-up. Nate's position isn't giving much away about his intentions, which can be useful if you have to throw a preemptive strike in self-defense.

The "powerslap" contacts with a cupped hand (not the fingers)and is dragged through the target by body rotation. It is an excellent pre-emptive knockout blow that can make a "street fight" very short indeed.

The palm can also be used to execute a hooking shot. This is sometimes called a "powerslap," but it is important to realize that the fingers are not used to strike with. Instead a slightly cupped hand is used, with the striking surface being the fleshy base of the palm. A strike of this nature is not very precise but it does not need to be; a solid contact along the base of the jaw is an excellent knockout blow that will not risk damage to the fighter's hands.

Hooked Punches

With all hooked shots, the principles are much the same. The "line up" is extremely important. A hooking strike should be thrown "through" the target, obtaining maximum weight transference from the fighter's positioning. Ideally, the fighters should not be positioned on a line from the centerline of one to the other. Greater impact is obtained by moving slightly in the direction of the hook so that the target point is inside the target.

Hooked strikes, by definition, have a shorter range than straight blows. It is possible to be beaten to the punch by a straight shot that comes in down the line left open by your hook. To avoid this, the strike is set up by doing something else first, often straight strikes that allow you to close the distance. A hook should be tight and short rather than a big swing, and should be launched without an obvious wind-up. Conversely, if you see an opponent's hand go out to the side, chances are he's about to launch a big, wild swing. While dangerous, this is less of a hazard than a tight hook thrown by someone who knows what he is doing.

The lead hand hook is difficult to master but can be devastating. It is thrown in a short, tight arc without significant wind-up. You will need

Poorly trained fighters will often "telegraph" their intentions to throw a hook with a huge chamber like this. The wild haymaker that is about to be launched will be powerful but slow and easy to avoid.

to move your lead hand out a little from guard, but not much. Keep the elbow up and line your forearm up along the line of the strike; a drooping elbow causes the strike to collapse and robs it of power. Twist the front foot inward as if crushing a cockroach underfoot and allow your body to turn into the hook. Snap back quickly to guard. The finishing position from a lead hand hook is a beautiful set up for an uppercut or body shot with the power hand.

The power hand hook is also thrown tightly and not in a huge arc, and can be a fight-ender. Lead hand hooks normally target the head but a power hand hook is equally useful against the short ribs or kidney area, and can

Keith (left) throws a straight lead-hand punch...

.... he returns to guard postion...

... and then throws a lead-hand hook, rotating the shoulder into the strike.

A hooked punch must be tight and disciplined. It is a fairly short-ranged shot that can find gaps in an opponent's guard. A hook is thrown with the whole body, not just the arm; twisting into the shot gives it additional power.

A body hook comes in under the guard. If you're in close, you can hit the kidney area from the side. At slightly longer distances the short ribs, or just in front of them, make a good target.

be thrown in a clinch. Hooks of all kinds can be used to get around a guard and are an excellent way to produce a knockout as they often come in from outside the opponent's field of vision. It is hard to roll with a punch that you don't see coming.

Uppercuts and Shovel Hooks

Uppercuts and shovel hooks (frontal body shots) use broadly the same mechanics as a hooked strike, but come down the centerline instead of around the side. The shovel hook is delivered with a "shovelling" action, into the opponent's diaphragm and solar plexus region. Anywhere along the base of the ribs will get results, and a perfect shot will crumple most opponents. To deliver maximum power, step in and push the power side hip forward as you deliver the strike.

The uppercut is difficult to execute effectively but is worth the trouble of learning to do properly. It allows a fighter to change his angle of attack and is often used to finish off an opponent who has been weakened by other blows. It comes up like a piston, under the opponent's jaw and is pushed through the target by the power of the fighter's legs.

To deliver a powerful uppercut, drop your weight slightly and bend your legs a little. Drive your fist up under the opponent's jaw and straighten

The shovel hook is a powerful body shot. It is unlikely to end a fight on its own, but a few good body blows will seriously impair the opponent's ability to fight and bring you closer to a victory.

The uppercut can be thrown with the lead or power hand. It is a close-range shot that will snap an opponent's head back and may cause an instant knockout. Uppercuts tend to be finishing moves and are set up using other strikes.

your legs and body to add impetus. A good uppercut can be delivered with either hand and will snap the opponent's head back. Uppercuts can also be delivered to an opponent who is bent over as the result of a body shot or a lead hand hook to the head.

Hammerfists

Hammerfists are delivered by straightening a bent arm and striking with the base of the fist. This is instinctive and very effective. Hammerfists can be dropped onto an opponent on the ground from a dominant position or used as part of your standup striking repertoire. Hammerfists can be delivered inward or outwards (or forehand/backhand if you prefer). In both cases, more power is generated by turning your body in the direction of the strike.

Note that a hammerfist is different to a backfist. The latter is delivered with the back of the hand and is intrinsically less powerful than a hammerfist. While spinning backfists may look impressive they are at best low-percentage moves and should be avoided. If you do find yourself in a position where a turning strike seems like a good option, a hammerfist can be delivered from almost anywhere that a backfist can, and it is a much more effective strike.

A hammerfist uses the base of the hand to land a very heavy strike that may come in from an unexpected angle. It has the advantage that the fleshy base of the hand protects it from damage.

A hammerfist can be used to attack the legs from the clinch. This is surprisingly painful and can reduce an opponent's mobility for the rest of the fight.

A fast, flicky backfist is a good way to score points in a competition, but it does little more than sting the opponent.

Striking with the back of the hand is also questionable; a poor contact can break several of the small bones in the hand.

Using Hooked Strikes

Hooked strikes are commonly used to change the line of attack and to seek a knockout on an opponent opened up by other blows. For example, you might throw a lead/cross combination, then step in slightly to deliver a lead hook around the opponent's guard which has been drawn onto the centerline to protect against your straight shots. The hook should knock him slightly sideways and open him up for an uppercut or shovel hook up the center.

An alternative is to exploit the opponent's expectations. Most fighters punch one-two-one-two with alternating hands, and the opponent will be expecting this. So, instead you throw a lead hand shot, move in slightly and follow with a fast lead hook before finally delivering the cross once the opponent has been opened up. With his guard positioned to meet the expected power hand shot, the opponent may be caught unawares by the hook.

Hammerfists can be used to "clear the line," sweeping an opponent's guard out of the way with a lead-hand hammerfist so that the power hand can follow through. They are more commonly used in groundfighting however. Hooked shots are also common in groundfighting and clinch work as they go around a guard and into vulnerable areas such as the side of the head or the floating ribs.

Hammerfists are excellent ground-and-pound tools that can be used to soften up an opponent for a submission attempt, or just beat him senseless.

Rick is making the most of his opportunity by dropping the strike from a good height...

... and using his bodyweight to add extra impact.

CHAPTER 7

Elbow Strikes

General Principles

Elbow strikes are arguably the most powerful of all "hand" strikes and can be thrown at very close quarters. The most common elbow strike is a hooking shot to the head or body, but thrusting, dropping, and rising elbows are all excellent close-quarters striking tools. Elbows are also useful on the ground as an adjunct to grappling skills.

The elbow is a very hard bone and is not prone to damage in the same way that hands are. Thus elbow shots can be delivered to "hard" targets such as the head without any worry of injuring yourself. The elbow is on the end of a short lever, i.e. it is connected to your body by your upper arm only, as opposed to a punch, which is at the end of the arm with joints

Elbow strikes can in many cases be thought of as a shorter version of hand strikes. A hooking elbow follows a similar path to a hook punch and uses similar body mechanics, though the arc is much shorter.

In a collision between skull and elbow, the head always comes off worst. There is no danger of damage to the striking point with an elbow strike.

between it and the attachment point. This means that there is very little "give" in an elbow strike. All the force goes into the target, with virtually none absorbed by your striking arm.

Elbows thus combine a hard striking point with a very powerful strike, but only if they are delivered properly. They are short-range striking tools and require considerable body movement to generate power.

Hooking Elbows

A hooking elbow is, to a great extent, a hook punch with the forearm and hand kept out of the way. The striking point is the bony end of the elbow; a badly thrown elbow will often strike with part of the forearm instead. This is not entirely ineffective but it wastes much of the potential of the strike. It is thus important to correctly judge the distance to the target.

To throw a hooking elbow, the shoulder is pushed forward and rotated into the strike much as in a hook punch. The forearm stays close to the body, with the hand rotated so that the back of your hand is facing you, thumb down. Target is usually the head but a body shot can also be effective.

A hooking elbow can also be thrown overhand, coming down into the opponent's collarbone region or head. This is useful in a clinch, where striking options can be limited by position and limbs in the way. Similarly, a rising elbow is an excellent substitute for an uppercut. It is thrown almost as if reaching over your shoulder to scratch your back, and brings the point of your elbow up under the opponent's jaw. While only useful at extreme close quarters, this is a punishing strike.

A hooking elbow strike can be thrown in a horizontal arc or overhand...

... it is a potent close-range follow-up to punches, especially if you can grab the opponent and pull him onto the strike.

It takes some practice to effectively deliver a rising elbow strike, but the effect of a hard bone under the jaw is worth the effort.

Hooking elbows are rarely thrown in isolation. Commonly, they are used as part of a combination or sequence of strikes. One option is to substitute an elbow where a hook punch might be used, to compensate for a change in range. Other fighters will deliberately close in during a sequence to try to deliver elbows. As short-range striking tools, hooking elbows are very much weapons of opportunity; it is worth spending some time working on strike combinations that include elbows so that you can incorporate them wherever they will be useful.

This technique really is best thought of as part of your general striking toolkit rather than something separate, allowing you to flow seamlessly from other hand strikes to elbows and back again as the opportunity presents itself.

Straight Elbows

A straight elbow comes out to the fighter's side or backwards. The elbow is driven point-first into an opponent, traveling in a straight line. This technique is a staple of many traditional martial arts, but is of questionable usefulness under many circumstances. There are, however, times when this technique can be used very effectively.

A straight elbow can be delivered one of two ways. If you are side-on to the opponent then you can draw your forearm across your chest, then drive it out. If he is behind you then the elbow is driven directly backwards. This is normally useful if you have been grabbed from behind or have ended up with your back to the opponent as the result of a takedown or during groundfighting. The same movement, more or less, is used to "pull" elbows

A straight elbow can be used as an offensive-defensive technique against an opponent who tries to close in for a grab or takedown attempt, or as a purely offensive movement.

into an opponent on the ground. This is often done from side control but strikes can be delivered any time the opportunity presents itself.

A straight elbow can also be delivered downwards, and is sometimes called a dropping elbow. There is nothing very scientific about this; raise your arm above the target and drive the elbow downwards into him. In a standing position, the collarbone area is vulnerable to this kind of strike,

Chris (right) knows where his opponent is, because contact is necessary for any sort of grip. As Keith tries to establish a rear naked choke, Chris chambers a rear elbow strike by extending his hand forward....

... and drives his elbow back into Keith's midsection. Chris is already starting to peel the grip off his neck before the strike has taken effect.

A dropping elbow to the collar-bone area is very much a strike of opportunity; if you find your-self in a position to deliver one, it will weaken the opponent and perhaps cause him to recoil, but it won't end a fight on its own.

or the opponent's back if he is bent over. A good target in that case is the lung area, under the shoulder blades. On the ground, elbows can be dropped in wherever there is the opening.

Defensive Elbows

Effective use of elbows can blur the line between offense and defense. For example, a movement almost identical to that used to deliver a rising

The opponent's fist or bicep might hit your elbow, but even if it doesn't you have protected yourself from his hook punch and set up a good position for an arm wrap or a one-handed head clinch.

It is possible to simply cover your head, but it is far more effective to move forward, inside the arc of the strike, to weaken it. This also has the effect of bringing you into clinch distance.

If you've been rocked by a shot, covering up and crashing in like this can prevent the opponent from taking advantage of the situation, and sets you up for a clinch which will minimize the damage you take while you collect your wits.

elbow puts your forearm along the side of your head to protect against a strike, and presents your elbow for the opponent to hit. If you're lucky, he will strike the hard bone and damage his hand; if not then at least you've covered the target area.

Another offensive-defensive use of elbows is to use a double head cover position as the opponent strikes, and lunge forward to crash into his chest with your elbows. This not only defeats his strike (it works best against hook punches) but delivers a painful strike and puts you at close quarters

Nate (left) prevents Gary from locking the clinch in by pushing his right elbow into Gary's chest, creating some distance to work with.

A sharp forward elbow strike into the chest has a similar effect.

Nate creates a strong structure to keep Gary at a distance by bracing his hand against his head. Pushing forward against Nate's elbow will be painful for his opponent and will not achieve much.

This time Nate uses both arms to break Gary's clinch and create some space...

... and takes advantage of the opportunity to land a short rising elbow strike to Gary's temple...

... which in turn sets up a more powerful elbow strike to the head.

for clinch work or a takedown. Elbows are one of the few striking tools where it is actually worth striking the chest; the hard points of your elbows will cause trauma to an opponent's chest muscles, weakening his arms. The strike also causes intense pain and may make the opponent recoil.

A straight elbow can be used defensively to make some distance. From a fairly typical guard position, with your hand higher than your elbow, drive the elbow directly forward and into the opponent's chest. You really cannot miss if he is close to you. The opponent may recoil or you can use the strike to set up something else, such as a head clinch.

Using Elbow Strikes

In many martial arts the elbow strike is used in an extremely stylized manner. This can involve taking a big step towards an opponent while turning sideways-on to him, then driving out the strike. There are reasons for this, which may be valid, but under most "fight" circumstances the strike simply will not land; people move in fights and it takes too long to deliver a blow in this manner.

Nate (right) performs an arm-drag take-down on Gary....

... slamming Gary into the floor and landing heavily on his ribs....

... and an elbow strike to the head which will keep Gary from doing much to resist as Nate turns over into a side control position.

Depending on the landing, a backwards elbow to the head is another good option, again followed by a turn into side control.

As a rule, elbows are delivered to a target that is already there, either because the opponent has closed in, or because an opportunity has presented itself in grappling. Elbows should also be an integrated part of your offensive striking repertoire, delivered instead of punches when the range closes. You may choose to use your longer strikes to get in close for elbows, or simply have them ready in case the range gets too short for other strikes.

Nate has established a right-handed collar tie and delivers an elbow strike to Gary's head with his left...

... then moves to his left, dragging Gary around to further disorient him as Nate changes hands on the clinch...

... now controlling Gary's head with his left hand, Nate chambers a right-handed elbow strike...

... and drops it in.

However, the best use of elbow strikes is to combine them with clinch work. You might use an elbow to set up a clinch, e.g. by striking the opponent in the side of the head with a hooking elbow, then grabbing him round the back of the head with the same arm. This is done with a sort of flipping motion, whereby your striking elbow stays where it landed and acts as a pivot to bring your hand around the back of the head. Pull the opponent to the side with this hand and deliver a strike with the opposite elbow.

... before re-establishing a right-handed clinch and moving to his right. Knee strikes or more elbows may follow, or a takedown attempt.

Having obtained a one-handed collar tie in this manner, you can keep banging elbows in with the same hand, or swap hands after each strike. Alternatively, you can use this technique to set up something different, such as a head clinch with knee strikes. The entry is much the same as above; fire an elbow into the opponent's head then flip the hand round the back of his head for a collar tie. Now slam in the other elbow and flip that hand into place. Pull the opponent's head down with what is now a Muay Thai style head clinch, and deliver knee strikes.

Other elbows can be used in the clinch, that is, you may be able to drop an elbow into the collarbone area if the opportunity presents itself. Or an elbow can be used to set something else up. You might find yourself with partial control of the opponent's right arm after covering a strike, and use this to pull yourself in for an elbow strike with your right arm, which then reaches past the opponent's head to pull him into a guillotine strike.

Effective fighters deliver shock and pain to the opponent at every opportunity, and elbow strikes are an excellent way of doing just that. You might be able to use one for a full-power finishing move, but even a short dig is painful and distracting, wearing down the opponents and disrupting whatever he is trying to do.

CHAPTER 8

Kicks and Knees

General Principles

Kicks are extremely powerful weapons, but they do have one significant drawback: they compromise your balance. When you lift one foot up, you do not lose 50% of your balance; it's more like 80%. Even if the kick is not caught, you are vulnerable while you get your foot back down and re-establish a good base. Kicks can and do end fights, but they must be used intelligently to avoid becoming counterproductive.

For example, if you land a good but not excellent kick and the opponent takes advantage of the fact that you have one foot off the ground to shoot in for a successful takedown, you have traded a single (albeit painful) strike for a highly disadvantageous position. This is not a good rate of exchange.

It may sound obvious, but lifting up a foot compromises your balance. Something as simple as a good hard shove can land you on your back. If you're going to kick at all, choose your moment and land a good one.

The side kick deserves an honorable mention here, although we decided not to include it in our 20 "must have" techniques. It is not quite as generally useful as push or roundhouse kicks and if it is not timed perfectly it can be easily countered.

Kicks to the head are spectacular, and good candidates for "Knockout of the Night" but they are hard to pull off and leave you open for a long time. Most fighters cannot deliver a head kick with the same force that they can kick the body or legs, so in general it is better to attack these targets and use your hands against the head; they're better positioned for it.

Kicking is always a risk. If this kick does not put me out of the fight then I should be able to shoot in for a single-leg takedown before my opponent can get his kicking foot back on the floor.

Kicks are often thought of as long-range striking tools, but they can also be used to close the distance and bring you into range for other strikes or a grappling attack.

Having delivered a front kick, I could move back out of range. But I'd rather get close and follow up. As my kicking foot drops to the floor I can lunge in for a head clinch while the opponent is still recovering from the kick to his midsection.

Knee strikes are subject to the same comments as kicks for the most part, though they have a shorter effective range and are best thrown from a clinch. However, they can be used as a "free" striking tool in the manner of a very short-range kick. Indeed, if you set up a roundhouse kick and find the range is too short, a roundhouse knee works just as well. Knee strikes are also useful on the ground.

There are many possible kicking techniques. Most are overly specialized or are low-percentage moves so we have included a very limited selection here. These will serve well in a range of circumstances and are worth developing to a good standard.

Straight Knee Strikes

The straight knee strike is a simple matter of lifting the knee up rapidly or driving it forwards. It is more a battering ram than a sniper's bullet, in that precision is not really necessary. Knees are effective against the head, body or legs and can be thrown "free" or in a clinch.

The ideal knee strike is performed from a Muay Thai style head clinch, pulling the opponent onto the strike. It is possible to knee to the head but a body strike is also effective. Do not knee with the front leg; this is weak. Instead take the striking leg well back and then drive it in hard. If you want to throw another, you can take the leg right back again for another long powerful strike, or put it down short and strike with the other knee.

Normally a close-in strike, a knee strike can be delivered with a jump forward, striking the body or head. Total commitment is required...

... but if timed right a "flying knee" strike can be devastating. If the opponent is still on his feet, you can land in a head clinch position and deliver more strikes.

It is not advisable to throw more than two straight knee strikes in succession, because the opponent will defend. He may jam your strike and try to grab the knee for a takedown, or might put his elbows down in the hope that you will hit them. Either way, it is wise to switch to a different strike (e.g. roundhouse knees or perhaps elbows) or a grappling technique. You can come back to knees again once he is distracted.

A straight knee can also be thrown as a "flying knee" or as a rapid attack. In either case, keep your hands up to protect your head and accelerate forward. The knee is driven in by the momentum of your forward lunge plus the torque of your entire body. For maximum impact, drive off the striking leg, stepping slightly forward with the other foot to bring you into range. Bring the striking knee up and point it at the target as your non-striking leg accelerates you forward. At the moment of impact, shoot your hands around the opponent's head for a clinch and get your feet on the ground. As soon as you're down, start firing more knees into his body.

Straight knees can be fired into the body and legs during a clinch, and are also useful on the ground. Knees can be especially effective from side control, whether you are on the top or bottom, and can be used to soften up an opponent for a submission or simply to pulverize him.

Roundhouse Knees

A roundhouse knee follows the path of a roundhouse kick to some extent. There are two ways to throw this technique. If you simply lift the knee, leaving your lower leg pointing downwards, you can swing it inwards and deliver a strike with the hard inside of your knee. This is most effective against the head; it is difficult to generate great power this way. It is an excellent way to open up an opponent in the clinch however; fire a couple of straight knees and he'll start to cover the center-line. Now you come around the sides, causing him to shift his defense. That opens up the centerline again.

A more powerful version of the roundhouse knee is performed by rolling your leg over so that the lower leg is behind the striking knee. This adds the weight of the leg to the impact of the strike and lines the hip up better; you can torque this one in with your whole body behind it.

A roundhouse knee of this kind is a little slower than a straight knee, and it does compromise your balance somewhat. However, it is a very powerful strike. Come in, slightly upwards, just under the ribs if you can; this can make breathing difficult for the opponent or crumple him up and make him vulnerable to whatever you feel like doing to him next.

The knee strike follows the same line as the lower leg...

... and drives in deep into the floating ribs. A solid head clinch is used to pull the strike into the opponent.

A roundhouse knee to the outside of the leg can weaken the opponent during vertical grappling or distract him while you set up your next move.

Push Kick

Perhaps the most basic of all kicks, a push kick delivers a lot of impact and can be used to stop an advancing opponent. It will drive the target backwards or fold him in the middle depending on where it lands. Push kicks are normally delivered off the rear foot but can be landed effectively, with some practice, using the front foot. A "snap" kick, as taught in many martial arts is painful but much less effective, as it relies on surface impact rather than driving into the target.

A push kick requires forward weight transference, meaning your whole body is moving forward as your foot impacts the target. If you can snap your foot back to chamber without losing your balance, it's not a push kick.

A push kick can be launched from a fairly long distance. For maximum power it comes from the back foot; in this case the right.

The push kick is exactly what the name says it is—it goes in deep and drives through the target...

... who should be shoved bodily backwards. Your kicking foot will then drop down in front of you, with all of its energy transferred to the target.

This is all wrong. Off-balance and badly chambered, there is little that can be achieved from here except a wild swing that lacks both aim and power.

The formal chamber looks stylized but you don't stand around in this position; it's something you pass through on your way to delivering a powerful kick that does not leave you over-committed, off-balance, and vulnerable.

The ball of the foot is most commonly used as a striking area, but sometimes the whole sole connects. It is important to maximize weight transference into the target by pushing the hips forward and down as your kick connects. This will stop an opponent's forward movement and can be delivered against the legs or body.

The push kick is chambered by lifting the knee of the kicking leg to the necessary height, then driving the kick forward by straightening the leg. Do

Blocking a kick by slamming your forearm into the opponent's leg is a good way to injure yourself, but a front kick can be deflected to the side with a sweeping or pushing action. You should also move sideways out of the path of the kick.

not swing the leg backwards as if kicking a football; if it helps, imagine that your leg is being lifted up by a string attached to the toes. Drive the kick into the target with forward momentum; for this reason a kick off the back leg generates more power. Do not snap the kick back to its chamber and put it back down behind you. Instead, use the kick to push the opponent off you and drop your foot to the floor in front of you, stepping forward with further strikes.

A push kick can be deflected, evaded or caught if the opponent sees it coming. Disguise your intent by feinting hand strikes or attack when the opponent is staggered by a sequence of strikes. In a pure kickboxing context (i.e. no grappling is permitted) the push kick provides a good clean finish to a sequence by sending the opponent staggering away from you. In MMA or self-defense, you might prefer to follow up with more strikes or a clinch.

Roundhouse Kick

Roundhouse kicks can be delivered with either leg, but it is much easier to generate power using the rear leg. The principle is the same either way; lift the knee up to point at the intended target, then straighten the leg violently while twisting the body into the strike. It is important to open up your hips by turning your non-kicking foot in the direction of the strike. This allows more power to be generated and avoids straining the knee.

The striking area is the shin or top of the foot, but a roundhouse kick can be shortened into a knee if the range changes. A kick to the outside of

A roundhouse kick goes where your knee is pointing, so obviously the knee has to be lifted high enough to allow the kick to reach your intended target. The other foot must be turned in the direction of the kick to allow proper rotation.

A roundhouse kick does not flick the target and then snap neatly back to chamber. It is fully committed and drives deep into the target. Do not worry about stopping the kick—the opponent's body or training equipment will do that for you.

A solid roundhouse kick will not only hurt the opponent, it will also buckle his leg or knock it out from under him, preventing him from retaliating.

the leg should come in slightly downwards and drive through hard, hoping to buckle the leg. The outside of the thigh can be conditioned to take a few kicks, but it is possible to chop down most opponents by repeatedly kicking the leg.

A roundhouse to the head is powerful but requires a lot of skill. It is not really worth putting in the time to develop this strike until you have mastered simpler and more commonly useable techniques, and you should not attempt it until you have obtained that skill—nothing will land you on your back faster than a badly executed head kick.

If kicking the body, coming in slightly upwards under the ribs is always good. Body shots like this can quickly degrade the opponent's ability to fight, but there is always the risk of the kick being caught. All the same, if you are going to kick at all then commit to it and drive it in hard. Do not flick the kick out and snap it back to chamber; smash it into the target. If you kick him hard enough, the opponent will not be able to catch your kick.

Using Kicks and Knees

Nervous fighters, who lack confidence, often try to use kicks to reach the opponent without coming too far into reach for a counterattack. Kicks of this sort tend to be thrown from too far away and lack both power and commitment. They waste energy, risk a counterattack, and perhaps worst of all they inform anyone who knows anything about fighting that you are scared and not willing to launch a proper attack. Fighters who nervously poke at their opponent like this actually make their opponent more confident and set up their own eventual defeat.

If you want your kicks to land and be effective, you have to get close enough to reach the opponent even if he tries to move back. A sudden, sharp move in can get you close enough, but you have to fully commit or not kick at all. Anything else is a waste of effort.

A kick that makes contact at the very end of its extension may look impressive but will not significantly harm your opponent. It is also relatively easy to evade long kicks, especially those thrown in isolation with no deception or set-up.

Kicks are an all-or-nothing weapon for most fighters. Some can and do use them as probing attacks like a boxer's jab, but for most fighters a kick should do heavy damage or not be thrown at all. The key to delivering this damage is weight transference; kicks should land hard and heavy, and drive into the target. Don't worry about keeping your balance while you retract the kick and put it down again; use the opponent's body to stop the kick and support you.

Generally speaking, it is relatively easy to see a kick that is thrown in isolation. If you try to cross a gap between you and the opponent with a kick, chances are he will avoid or counter it. It is thus much better to set up a kick, perhaps with hand strikes or by movement, than to simply throw it out and hope for the best. An element of deception, such as moving in while chambering the hands for a punch combination, can serve to conceal your intention to kick.

The lead-leg roundhouse is a good opening move, especially against an opponent who expects you to close in for hand strikes. It is best applied aggressively against the inside of the opponent's lead leg. The aim point is the inner thigh, just above the knee. This causes the leg to buckle outwards and breaks the opponent's balance. As your leg recoils from the impact, use this to drop it rapidly back to the ground and propel you inwards for a cross or elbow strike.

Correctly "reading" his opponent's intentions, Nate (right) recognizes a powerful trailing-leg roundhouse kick about to come in...

... wanting none of it, he moves back out of reach. By the time the opponent has begun to chamber his kick, it has already failed...

... and is aborted. Now Nate has an opportunity to counterattack as his opponent puts down the foot he intended to kick with.

The lead leg roundhouse kick to the inner thigh is extremely painful and buckles the leg outwards. It can be used as a single shot when the opportunity arises, or as an opening move to close the distance.

The trailing leg roundhouse can sometimes be used in isolation or as an opening move but it is more likely to land if used as a finisher on the end of a sequence. The classic combination is a lead-cross with the hands, followed up with a roundhouse kick to the body or legs. The hand strikes pull the opponent's attention and guard up, and then you go in underneath.

Knees are, as noted elsewhere, weapons of opportunity. They can be used to draw his attention away from your attempts to improve a clinch situation by changing hand position, or to weaken an opponent for a take-down. Knees can be driven into the opponent any time you find yourself close enough. Even if you do not obtain a finish this way, you can weaken your opponent's body and will with constant attacks.

From a two-handed Thai clinch, Nate (left) chambers a knee strike...

... and drives it into the opponent's quadriceps, weakening his leg...

... which makes him unable to resist being pulled down...

... and dumped face-first onto the mats.

CHAPTER 9

Leg Takedowns

General Principles

As with all takedowns, there are two stages to a leg takedown: the entry and the takedown itself. The entry is what gets you into a position to perform the takedown without being struck by the opponent or prevented from making your takedown attempt. It may or may not be fair to say that the entry is the most important part of a takedown, but without a good entry you will not be able to even make the attempt. A good entry will often either exploit an opening given to you by the opponent or else will deceive him about your intentions.

For example, you might shoot in for a takedown under a high kick. In this case the entry serves both to protect you from the kick (it goes over you) and also to get you into position to take the opponent down. This kind of exploitation of an opening has the advantage that the opponent is committed to something that may well compromise his ability to defend. Alternatively, you might throw a lead hand punch as a deception. The opponent will probably expect a cross to follow, i.e. a high punch. Instead you change the level and shoot in low while his attention is on the high line.

Having successfully entered, the takedown is a matter of establishing the right grip or position and executing the technique. Generally speaking, two points of contact are needed for a successful takedown. If you push an opponent's head backwards, he can step back and regain his balance. If you pull his leg away from under him, he can base out or shift his balance. His chances of staying upright are greatly diminished if you push his head back and take away his foot from under him at the same time.

Nate (right) sets up a takedown by distracting me by shooting out his hand. It's a simple deception but it gets my attention for an instant...

... so his deep shoot catches me completely by surprise.

I can't react in time to prevent a takedown...

... and so I begin my journey floorwards.

Nate gets control of my leg by wrapping it with his arm. He could apply an Achilles tendon lock at this point...

... but he's got other ideas, moving around to the side where he can do me a lot of damage. His right knee drops onto my ribs to prevent me escaping.

Two points of contact make even very simple takedowns effective. A sweeping edge-of-foot kick to the opponent's leg coupled with a firm pull on his head ...

... is enough to overbalance him. This is not a "sweep" by the way, it's a kick that does damage then follows through to push the leg away.

There are three possible reasons for executing a takedown:
- To get the opponent on the ground for groundfighting
- To smash the opponent into the ground to cause harm
- To cause his bodyweight to break a locked joint as he falls

These are by no means exclusive, though for obvious reasons the third option is more applicable to self-defense than to a competition environment. You should try to get as much out of a takedown as possible. Even if you intend to look for a finish on the ground, making the opponent land hard can weaken him or prevent him from resisting for a moment, while you establish a good position. Thus, while it is generally wise to train takedowns at less than full intensity most of the time (to avoid injury), your aim when making a takedown attempt "for real" is to dump the opponent so hard that you do not need to follow up.

The Shoot

The standard entry for a leg takedown is the "shoot." This is a rapid forward movement ending in a low position ready to grab the opponent by one or both legs. A single-leg takedown does not require such a deep entry

Starting from just outside his opponent's hitting range, Chris (right) makes the decision to shoot in.

Chris drops into a crouch but does not start moving forward until he is already down low.

as a double-leg, but either way it is important to get your center of gravity low, and to stay under the opponent's high-line strikes such as punches to where your head would normally be.

Many fighters use a diagonal down-and-in shoot from a typical upright guard position. This has the advantage of being unexpected; the opponent cannot know whether you are going to kick, punch, or shoot from this position. So if you can disguise your intent until you make the shoot, the opponent will have little time to react. On the downside, it is easier to stop a down-and-in diagonal shoot than a down-then-in horizontal one if it is spotted in time.

By crouching low then shooting in horizontally, you come in lower and, usually, deeper. This makes the takedown more likely to succeed. However, it takes longer to set up this kind of shoot; the opponent may have time to react unless you catch him off guard. In both cases, you are extremely vulnerable if your shoot or takedown attempt fails. You must fully commit to the attempt or not try at all; anything in between will end badly for you.

The Single Leg Takedown

There are several ways to perform a single-leg takedown, some of them quite different from the others. The common principle is to push the opponent backwards while taking away his lead leg by lifting it up.

From your guard position, get low and shoot in deep, driving the opponent's hip backwards to break his posture. There are arguments both ways about whether your head goes to the "inside" or the "outside;" both have their merits. If your head is inside, it is used to push the opponent's hip

The only problem with a "down-then-in" shoot like this is that it is necessary to commit while still quite far from the opponent, which may give him time to react. Speed and surprise are essential.

Starting at much the same distance, Chris moves forward and down at the same time. This has the effect of disguising his intentions for a little longer.

The end result of a "down-and-in" shoot of this sort is much the same, but this version is a bit more quick-and-dirty.

This is what happens if you don't get down low enough. It's not a shoot at all; it's a waist tackle. There are still options from here if you can establish a body lock, but in reality a tackle of this sort is fairly easy to counter.

Grab the opponent's leg and hug it tightly to your body, driving his hip back with your shoulder.

Alternatively, fold the hip by pushing with your forearm and lift from the ankle. If you try to lift from the knee instead, the takedown will probably fail and you may well receive a knee strike for your trouble.

back along with your shoulder. If the head goes outside, push with your shoulder and arm.

At the same time, grab the opponent's leg and lift it up. Some fighters prefer to grab the ankle with one hand and pull up-and-forward, others grab the leg with both hands just above the knee, lifting it up and hugging it to their body as they push the opponent back.

The key in either case is to get one of the opponent's legs off the ground while forcing his hip back. It is vital to drive through with commitment, pushing yourself forward with your rear leg.

The Double Leg Takedown

Shoot in deep and grab the opponent round the backs of his legs. Your head goes to the outside in this case, and it is mainly your lead shoulder that pushes the opponent back. Drive hard forward with your rear foot and pull the opponent's legs toward you.

If you simply hold the opponent's legs and push him back, he will probably fall. But to get the most out of this takedown, try to scoop up his legs as if you were going to put your hands into your hip pockets. The more horizontal you can get the opponent, the harder he will fall.

*Grab the opponent
around the backs of
the knees with a sharp
scooping or chopping
action, then pull up
and towards you.*

Using Leg Takedowns

It is entirely possible to simply shoot in from wherever you happen to be and take the opponent off guard. However, the odds of a successful takedown are increased if you set up first by drawing the opponent's attention upwards, like with a lead hand strike. A sudden change of level can catch an otherwise wary opponent by surprise and allow you to take him down.

Leg takedowns can be used from a clinch or a failed body lock takedown (covered in a later chapter), or as a response to a kick or knee. In the latter case, it you may catch a kick or knee while trying to defend against it, and find yourself positioned for a single leg takedown. If going from a clinch or other close-quarters situation it is necessary to move very suddenly; if you give away your intention you may run into a rising knee or find your takedown attempt jammed.

While leg takedowns are highly effective, they do have the drawback that often you will end up in the opponent's guard. If at all possible, throw his legs to the side and get around into side control or a standing position above the opponent's side. Many fighters will accept that they are going down and try to make the best of it by pulling guard on the way down. A vigorous takedown helps prevent the opponent from getting you under control, and if he lands hard you may get a second chance to pass or escape his guard before he collects his wits and begins defending properly.

Keith (right) prepares to throw a round-house kick. Mark makes a tough decision....

... and lunges in to weaken the kick, jamming it with his arms to prevent it developing any real force.

Mark is now well positioned to use a hip-and-ankle leg takedown on Keith, whose balance is already compromised.

CHAPTER 10

Reaping Takedowns

General Principles

Reaping takedowns get their name from the movement used to take the opponent's foot out from under him. It is said to resemble the action of cutting corn with a scythe. Note that these takedowns are not "foot sweeps" as taught in some martial arts. Sweeps only work against an opponent who is "light" on the swept foot and require perfect timing to take away a foot as the opponent is lifting it or just as he puts it down. Attempting to sweep a firmly planted foot usually results in a relatively weak kick to the ankle which does not achieve much other than some pain and annoyance.

A good reaping takedown, on the other hand, will demolish even a well based opponent, and can cause him to fall very hard. The principles of inner

The principles are the same for all reaping takedowns. Anchor your hand on the opponent's shoulder and use the forearm to push his head up and back. This will break his balance and cause him to fall when you take away one of his feet.

It is critical to move in deep when performing a reaping takedown. In the case of the outer reaping takedown you need to move almost past the opponent. Reaching in or trying to push him simply doesn't work. Commit fully and make it happen, or don't try at all.

This is one of the common errors with reaping takedowns. Nate (right) has not pushed Rick's head back and broken his balance. Worse, he has wrecked his own posture by trying to reach through with his foot instead of pushing forward with his whole body.

Rick (left) pushes Nate back by powering through with his blocked punch, and with one foot off the floor there's only one possible outcome...

and outer reaping takedowns are much the same; the opponent's balance is broken by pushing his head back, and one leg is take out from under him. There are many variations on these takedowns, those presented here are a simple and generic starting point.

As a general rule, a reaping takedown attacks the lead foot and can only work against an opponent who is off balance. The commonest mistake with these techniques is to reach in with the foot in the hope of hooking a leg away. Occasionally this does actually work, but more commonly it results in disaster as the fighter breaks his own balance and is dumped on his back. The key, as with most grappling techniques, is to establish a position from which the takedown can work before attempting it.

Outer Reap

Also known as a "rear trip" or "judo trip," the outer reap can be performed at time you have both your hands on the same side of the opponent's centerline. For example, if you have jammed a hook punch with both arms, the outer reap is already set up for you. If you are on the centerline, say in a Muay Thai style clinch, you need to move off center to be able to perform an outer reap. Go to the side of the opponent's lead foot; if he is square on, give him a shove to make him step back with one foot to base himself, then attack the other.

Nate (right) steps into Rick's hook punch, jamming it with a two-handed block...

... then pushes Rick's head up and back with an elbow under the chin, gripping Rick's shoulder to support the movement.

Nate continues to move in, pushing Rick's head back as he moves around the outside and starts to hook his right leg around Rick's.

With Rick's balance broken, his weight is heavily on his right leg. Nate takes it away...

... and Rick falls. Nate stays in close, ready to apply a submission or start dropping strikes.

Your outer arm should control the opponent's arm, by wrapping it or gripping his triceps. Your inner arm is used to tip his head back and break his balance. You can push up under his chin with your hand (ideally, land a short palm strike on the chin and then continue the upwards movement) or use your forearm. In this case, grip the opponent's trapezius and use it as a pivot to raise your elbow and forearm under his jaw. You need his head far enough back that his back arches for a successful takedown.

As you tip the head back, step in deep, pushing the opponent back with body-to-body contact as you step around his lead foot. Your foot then sweeps backwards, "reaping" his supporting leg as you project his head back. The bigger your reaping motion, the harder he will fall.

Keep hold of the opponent's arm as he falls, preventing him from landing away from you. You want him as close as possible. You may or may or may not be able to get an armlock on the arm you are holding, but you can certainly immobilize it. Drop your knee onto his ribs and start delivering strikes, or transition into a position for a submission.

Inner Reap
The inner reap is performed from directly in front of the opponent. Again, you attack his lead foot and should trap the arm on the same side to prevent him from simply stepping away. Push his head back and step in deep, hooking your leg around his lead leg from the inside and reaping it away. It is also possible to wrap his leg from the outside and push him

Rick (left) chambers a big swinging punch, creating a perfect opening. The inner reap can be performed from many other entries.

Nate (right) jams the punch, making sure his weight is moving forward to stop it. If he simply stood and took it, he might be driven back and pushed off balance.

Nate (right) continues to drive forward, pushing Rick's arm back. His own right forearm goes across Rick's throat and pushes up and back.

Nate moves in, sliding his right foot between Rick's feet and preparing to hook away Rick's left leg.

With his balance broken and one foot hooked out from under him, Rick begins to fall. Nate keeps control of Rick's arm on the way down.

over, falling on top of him; this is sometimes an alternative when you are prevented from going down the middle.

An inner reaping takedown will almost always land you in the opponent's guard if you go down with him. This is common; most fighters will hang on to you to try to stay upright. If you release your grip on him and shove him down once he's falling you may be able to stay upright or step over his legs, but this is not guaranteed.

It is sometimes possible to stay upright after an inner reaping takedown, but more commonly the opponent will drag you down with him, either deliberately or in an attempt to stay upright or at least soften his fall.

An experienced opponent will usually "pull guard" in this situation, quite possibly obtaining a closed guard even before he has hit the ground. The outer reap generally results in a harder fall and a batter position, but you have to take what you can get.

Using Reaping Takedowns

The outer reap offers a good combination of accessibility and power. It is easy to perform and gives both a hard landing for the opponent and a good position for you, but it does require an off-center position, which is not always available. The easiest entry is from jamming a hook punch but it is also possible to force your way or to use a variation of this technique to take down an opponent whose kick you have caught. Obviously, in this case you take away the leg he still has on the ground while tipping him backwards. This results in a very hard fall, especially if you reap his leg away vigorously.

The inner reap is very accessible from almost any clinch situation, and can be used to peel off an opponent who has grabbed you. Trap his arm and work your other hand to the centerline, pushing upwards until you reach his chin, and push it up and back. As he is bent backwards, the opponent may let go of you. If so, you can shove him back and follow up with a barrage of strikes. If he clings on, reap his lead leg and dump him in his back.

CHAPTER 11
Other Takedowns

General Principles

There are essentially three ways to obtain a takedown. One is to simply move in, establish the right grip and perform the takedown. A good example of this is shooting in for a double-leg takedown. Another way is to respond to something the opponent does to set up a takedown, like catching a kick or jamming a punch.

The third option is to grab the opponent anyway you can and "trade up" your grip by working towards a more advantageous position until you can make the takedown attempt. This often happens when you are in a clinch or instinctively grab an opponent as part of a punch defense. In this situation you may not have a useful grip, but any grip is better than none. If you can immobilize one of the opponent's limbs and limit his options, it is usually best to keep hold and advance your position from there rather than letting go and trying for a more effective grip.

"Trading up" your grip is best combined with close-quarters strikes to keep the opponent from reacting effectively and to wear him down. Once you have established the position you want, a takedown can follow.

Outer Wheel Takedown

From a frontal clinch position where you have an underhook on one side, "pop" the opponent's arm upwards with a sudden movement (this is more of a slap than a push; it needs to be sudden) and duck underneath. Your other hand goes around behind his head so that the bony inside of your wrist lies along the side of his neck. Reach up and grab your hand or wrist and lock in tight, placing your ear on his shoulder to protect yourself.

From an initial nobody's-winning-here weak clinch position...

... Nate (right) prepares to "pop" his opponent's arm upwards.

The movement is a sharp upwards slap, not a steady push.

The opponent's grip is dislodged and his arm pushed sharply upwards. Nate ducks his head and moves forward...

... passing the arm and coming up on the far side in a good position for an outer wheel or a body lock takedown.

From a clinch position...

... Nate (right) "pops" the opponent's arm up and ducks through...

... coming up behind the arm with a tight grip on the opponent's neck. Nate presses his ear to the opponent's shoulder to protect his head and to keep the grip locked in tight.

After establishing a solid hold, Nate rotates and drags his opponent down...

...landing in a dominant position with a solid hold still on the opponent's neck.

The position you have established applies a painful strangle and might be sufficient to obtain a tap. If not, you can take the opponent down easily enough from here. Pivot your outer foot backwards, rotating the opponent into the space you have just vacated while pulling him down. If you keep hold you will follow him to the ground in a reasonably advantageous position, but it is usually better to let go about halfway down and throw your opponent into the ground, then establish a knee-on position on his ribs to control him.

Body Lock Takedowns

From a frontal clinch position, or after closing in to protect yourself from a barrage of hook punches, grab the opponent around the lower back and lock your grip in tight, pulling his hips forward and against you to break his balance. From here, you can take him down by simply stepping forward. This is a front body lock takedown.

Many fighters will step in to establish the position with their right foot forward, then step around the outside of the opponent's legs with their left. As the opponent falls, the right leg is brought through to establish a mount position. For a more destructive takedown, it is possible to hook

The key to a side body lock takedown is a good grip around the floating ribs. If you drag the opponent in tight vigorously enough, he may start to fall even before you intend him to.

Sometimes you can't get a takedown right away, especially if the opponent resists vigorously. Lock the grip in tight, which restricts his breathing, and wait for the right moment as he tires or makes a mistake.

one of the opponent's legs away with your foot, or to pull his hips up and forward quite violently, then dump him hard.

For a side body lock takedown, pop the arm up as described for the outer wheel, or duck under a wild hook punch and come back up behind the opponent's arm. Your arm goes around the opponent at floating ribs level, and can be slammed into him for a strike. Use the inner bony part of the wrist for both the strike and the lock. Your other arm goes around the opponent's back as you move around to his side, so that you are chest-to side.

Lock your grip in by grabbing your own wrist or hand, and pull hard towards you. This squeezes the opponent's diaphragm and internal organs. From here, lift him up a little using your legs (don't lift with your back) and tip him over. You can sweep his foot out or knee him in the leg to help with this, but it is not always necessary. Once he is tipped sideways and has begun to fall, hurl him downwards to maximise the impact.

It is also possible to perform a very similar takedown from behind. Instead of moving to the opponent's side, continue right around so that you are chest to back. Grip him firmly around the middle then lift, tip and dump.

Clinch Takedowns

There are two very easy takedowns from a Muay Thai style clinch. Both work from a two-handed collar tie. You must keep your elbows down and a tight grip on the opponent for both. Pull the opponent's head down and deliver some knee strikes. If he begins to sag forward, help him on his way by stepping back while keeping tight hold of his head, pulling him down and forward. As he falls, throw him face-first into the ground.

From a two-handed head clinch, Nate (right) delivers a knee strike to the body, weakening his opponent and causing him to start to crumple.

Using the backward momentum of his leg, returning after the strike, Nate takes a long step backward and hauls his opponent's head forward and down.

As the opponent falls, Nate helps him on his way, dumping him face down on the ground.

For a (very) slightly more scientific takedown, instead of pulling straight down, pivot one leg back and rotate the opponent in the same direction, pulling forward, sideways and down. Keep dragging him down for as long as you can, then fling him into the floor. He should land close to you and well positioned for a knee-on position and a finish.

This time, instead of stepping straight back, Nate rotates and drags his opponent's head into the space he has just vacated...

... causing the opponent to land heavily on his back.

Using These Takedowns

These takedowns are sometimes "given" to you by what the opponent does or follow on logically from something you have just done. The clinch takedowns are an ideal follow-up to a series of knee strikes to the body, while a clinched opponent who tries to pull himself upright and out of your grip can be attacked with a front body lock or outer wheel takedown.

From a clinch position, Nate (right) decides to establish underhooks as a setup for his next move.

He suddenly moves sharply back to open up some space, and before the opponent can react...

... he drives his arm inside and under the opponent's...

... driving back in close to lock in the underhooks.

These takedowns can also be used defensively. You might go under a wild right hook and find yourself ideally positioned for an outer wheel or side/rear body lock takedown. Or you might get tagged and close in, grabbing the opponent anyhow you can to try to control him while you collect your wits. From there you might be presented with an opportunity for a front body lock takedown.

From a clinch position, these takedowns give you some good options. One underhook can be traded up for a side body lock or outer wheel by popping the arm and moving through. Double underhooks will give you a front body lock takedown, and if that fails you can drop into a quick-and-dirty double leg attempt. A one-handed head clinch can be used to deliver some "dirty boxing" strikes until you can establish a good two handed clinch and make the takedown.

Nate (right) closes in, attempting to establish double underhooks.

His opponent reacts in time, keeping Nate at a distance so that he cannot lock in the underhooks...

... so Nate continues his drive forward, taking a lower grip for a quick double-leg takedown attempt.

CHAPTER 12
Submissions and Destructions

General Principles

All of the techniques known as "submissions" were originally developed to cause damage or even death to an opponent. Indeed, one of the reasons why fighters submit is to avoid serious consequences. It is important to remember that these techniques are dangerous when training. Some fighters become complacent when just whacking on yet another armbar, but it only takes one mistake to put a training partner out of commission for a long time.

Similarly, while it is necessary to train to resist submissions, you cannot apply and resist at full intensity all the time or you will spend more time injured than not. As a rule, all submissions should be learned with a compliant training partner until they can be applied quickly and with confidence but with good control. After this, it is still wise to tap out as soon as the opponent "has it" rather than waiting until the pain is unbearable. Full-intensity training is necessary from time to time, but taking every fight to the last ditch is counterproductive; you will end up with permanently damaged joints.

Conversely, it is necessary to develop a suitable mindset for using submissions. You need to be comfortable with what you are doing to your opponent and willing to do it. Taking liberties with a training partner or opponent is unacceptable, but you do need to be willing to apply submissions hard and painfully if they are going to work. This mentality is developed by training submissions until they are second nature—not just the technical aspects but the willingness to put a joint lock or choke on and keep it there until the opponent taps.

It sometimes possible to lock in a submission hold "on the fly" but a methodical approach will get a result far more often. So you will need to get a grip on your opponent, trade up for a better one if necessary, then establish the position you need for your submission. Then, and only then, will you be able to lock in a successful position.

"Position before submission" works both ways. It is obviously good advice to the attacker, but it is also a broad hint to the defender. There are many submissions that cannot be escaped once they are locked in, but if you can prevent the opponent getting a good position, then he will not be able to submit you. Even if a submission hold is partially on, it is sometimes better to defend by attacking the opponent's position rather than trying to break his hold.

Many of these submissions are performed from side control, and for the sake of clarity we need to define which of your hands is which when in this position. Depending which side of the opponent you are on, one of your hands will be nearer his head than the other. We will call this your "head" hand. The one that's nearer his waist is your "waist" hand.

The Bar Choke/ Rear Naked Choke

The bar choke is the simplest of all chokes. It is normally performed against an opponent who is on his back. Place your forearm across the opponent's

It is quite rare for a one-handed choke like this to submit an opponent, but it does restrict his breathing and control his head while you set up something more certain to succeed... or hit him with your other hand.

Force one arm under the opponent's head to set up a better choke....

... then bring your arms together to create a guillotine effect. Add body weight to make the choke even tighter.

The rear naked choke uses the bony forearm just the same as the bar choke. The
forearm is forced under the opponent's
chin...

... and the other arm comes through
ready to lock it in.

The hand of the choking arm rests inside
your elbow and your other hand goes on
top of or behind the opponent's head.

The choke is applied by pushing the
opponent's head forward and down as
well as pulling in with your choking arm.

windpipe and push the bony part into his throat. This can be done one-handed against an opponent who has his back to the ground or a wall, by gripping his shoulder or trapezius with your hand and pushing your elbow forward. However, it is fairly easy to break this choke, so it is best used as a distraction or to immobilize an opponent for strikes.

For a much stronger choke, put your arm around the back of the opponent's head and grip your wrist or upper arm, then try to bring the elbow

Gary has taken his opponent's back during groundfighting. He gets an arm around his opponent's throat...

... and rolls onto his back, pulling his opponent in tight and locking the choke in with his other hand. Gary has also "hooked" his opponent with his legs to prevent escape.

There's nothing much to do from this position but tap out. A choke like this may cause unconsciousness in a few seconds, and will kill if not released promptly.

It is vital to release all submissions immediately the opponent taps out, even if you don't think it's "on" properly. The opponent may know something you don't!

of the choking arm to the gripping hand. If he is on his back, you can get your body weight into the choke by pushing your chest down onto your choking arm.

The rear naked choke or "RNC" is basically a bar choke from behind. It can be applied against any opponent who has his back to you, standing or on the ground. One way to take the opponent's back is to pop his arm and slip under it as per the outer wheel takedown. You might spot an opportunity to spin around behind the opponent while fighting on the ground or alternatively you might simply find yourself behind him as the result of a mistake.

However you get there, the choke is applied by placing yourself tightly chest-to-back and forcing your forearm across his throat. It is locked in place by pushing your other arm forward over his shoulder. Place the hand of your choking arm in the crook of your elbow and perform what is basically a bicep curl, placing your hand on the back of the opponent's head. The choke is applied not by pulling your choking arm towards you but by pushing his head forward and down. By forcing everything together you close up the gap under his chin with your arm in it; for a good choke you should squeeze, not pull.

The Triangle Choke

A triangle choke uses the opponent's arm and shoulder to compress the carotids and cut off blood supply to the brain. It can be performed from various positions, but for now we will consider just two; side control and the mount.

Establish side control without putting your hand under the opponent's head. If you try to get hold of his arm, he will normally assume that you are trying to obtain a Kimura or Americana and fight to keep his hand off the ground. Push his arm towards his head and reach past it with your head arm so that it is behind the triceps. Pull your head arm back as if elbowing someone behind you, and you will take the opponent's arm across his throat. Now scoop your arm under his head and push it through. Bring your waist hand up and lock the position in. Now simply squeeze.

From the mount, the choke is applied the same way. Push the opponent's arm across his throat and lean forward, pushing it down with your body weight. Feed your arms under his head and grab your elbows, then squeeze it all together; as if hugging your opponent to death.

From guard, the same principles apply. Push the opponent's arm across his body and pull his head down. Do not allow him to sit up or the choke will come off. It is sometimes possible to simply pull the opponent down on top of you with your arms and obtain a submission this way, but a

I've got side control but Nate (bottom) is determined not to let me have that arm for a Kimura or Americana.

I push Nate's arm back, under my arm-pit, and force my left arm past it so that his arm is behind my triceps.

I then pull my left arm back, keeping it close to my side, and slide it under his head. This traps his own arm across his throat.

Now I bring my hands together and squeeze everything, keeping my weight well down to avoid an attempt to reverse the position. Even with a submission hold in place you haven't won until the opponent taps out.

From the other side: I get his arm behind my triceps and push it across his throat by simply drawing my own arm back…

My hand goes under Nate's head in a sort of scooping action, locking his arm in place.

I push through to tighten the choke, and begin to bring my hands together. This is important—until I get my hands firmly locked together, the choke can be loosened by the opponent's struggles.

tighter grip is possible with the legs. Hook your leg over the opponent's back and lock it in by placing the opposite leg over your foot (with the foot in the bend of your knee) then pulling that leg back to tighten the hold.

Gary (top) pushes his opponent's arm across his throat, pressing down to hold it in place.

Gary's right arm goes under the opponent's head as he drops body weight onto the opponent's trapped arm to keep it in place. His left arm also feeds under the opponent's head.

Gary grabs the opponent's wrist, possibly applying a wristlock against the ground, but this is just a bonus. The choke is applied by squeezing the arms together with bodyweight on top.

The Guillotine Choke

The guillotine choke can be used in either a standing position or in groundwork. In both cases, the opponent's head is trapped under your armpit by wrapping your arm over his head then under his chin while he is facing towards you. As with other chokes, application is a matter of squeezing rather than pulling. Thus, rather than just pulling up on the forearm across

Keith (bottom) pushes his opponent's arm across so that both arms are on the same side of Keith's head. This sets up a triangle choke and incidentally prevents Chris from establishing a controling grip around Keith's head.

Keith brings his hands together and begins to squeeze. The choke is partially on at his point, but not fully. It is mainly applied by the opponent's trapped arm, i.e. Chris is feeling this mainly on the right side of his neck.

Keith closes his guard and locks in the choke. He can intensify it by arching his back and stretching Chris out.

his throat, you also push his head forward and down by dropping your shoulder. The movement can best be described as trying to snap his head off.

If performed from standing, the position is established by reaching over the opponent's shoulder from an "outside" position, that is, both your hands are on the same side of his head. Reach right through then use the weight of your arm to bring his head down by swinging it in an arc as if you were bringing your hand to your hip pocket. Force your forearm under his chin and lock in the position by grabbing your forearm or hand. There are several variations on this position, but in the chaos of a fight you will have to take what you can get rather than searching for the ideal position. Once locked in, push down with your shoulder and pull up with your arms, pushing your hips forward as if you were trying to lift the opponent up by his throat.

Gary (left) pulls his opponent's head down, perhaps assisted by a body shot, and loops his arm over the opponent's head.

Gary locks the choke in by forcing his arm under the opponent's throat, then bringing his hands together and establishing a firm grip.

He then pushes his hips up and forward, holding the opponent's head down with his armpit and pulling up with his arm on the throat. The opponent's own bodyweight adds to his discomfort.

On the ground, the guillotine is normally used on an opponent who is in your guard. Sit up and reach through as above. Pull his head down and lock in the choke, then stretch him out by arching your back and pushing with your legs. In both cases, be aware that this choke puts a lot of strain on the neck. Care should be taken in training for this reason, and also because unconsciousness can occur very quickly.

Gary (bottom) lunges up and to the side, forcing his right arm past the opponent's head...

... and using it to pull him down.

Gary pushes his arm under the opponent's throat and locks in the choke by gripping his arm with the other hand.

He applies the choke by pushing down with his legs and pulling towards his own head and chest with the choking arm, stretching the opponent out. He tries to arch his back and push his shoulders into the mat, but the opponent will tap long before that happens.

The Arm Bar

The straight arm bar can be applied from various positions on the ground and standing. The principles are the same in all cases; the arm is isolated to prevent the opponent defending, and then is straightened out with something behind the elbow to act as a fulcrum. This causes intense pain and can break the joint unless the opponent submits. The opponent must of course be prevented from escaping by holding him in a vulnerable position.

From the mount position, Gary has grabbed his opponent's straight arm and retains it as he moves around to the side.

He hugs the arm to his chest as he moves into a 90-degree position. His left leg comes round, ready to swing across the opponent's head.

Gary drops his weight back and holds his opponent down with his legs, pushing up with his hips to drive the opponent's elbow upwards and apply the joint lock.

The classic arm bar is performed from the mount position. Drop a few shots into the opponent's head to get him to give you an arm—the straighter, the better. Grab the arm and hug it to your body to prevent him taking it back. Keeping the arm in place, Sweep out your leg and spin around the arm you are holding so that you are at 90 degrees to the opponent. Your leg goes over his face to hold him down as you drop backwards.

In practice, hold the arm quite loosely as you make this transition to avoid accidental injury, and only apply the lock properly after you are firmly on the ground. With more practice you can learn to put the lock on hard and fast without causing damage. To apply the lock once on the ground, push up with your hips as you pull the arm into your chest. Your groin should be as close to the opponent's armpit as possible, while your grip will be on the wrist.

Gary forces his hand under the opponent's more-or-less straight arm while holding it in place with his other hand. If the opponent manages to bend his arm very much, this technique will not succeed.

Gary locks his position by gripping his own arm while pushing down and straightening the opponent's arm.

An arm bar can also be applied from side control against an opponent whose arm is straight out sideways, perhaps trying to defend against a Kimura or Americana (see below). Pin the arm you are attacking down, with the palm up. Slip your other hand under the arm and grab your wrist so that your arm is behind the opponent's elbow. Now push down on his wrist while keeping your weight on his chest to prevent escape.

The Kimura and Americana (Reverse Kimura)

Both of these techniques attack the shoulder and can cause severe damage if cranked on hard. They require the opponent to be immobilized to be effective, but can be used from several different positions.

Establish a solid side control position, holding the opponent down with chest-to-chest bodyweight. Grab his wrist with your waist hand and hold it down. His palm must be down. Place your head hand palm down on the mats to make a ramp and push his arm up the ramp, sliding through underneath. You want to be as close to his elbow as possible. Lift the fingers of your head hand up to make a trap and bring your waist hand to the trap. Close the trap by grabbing your waist-hand wrist firmly.

Some fighters will come up to one knee to get leverage for a Kimura, but this can sometimes allow the opponent to sit up and escape. Instead, move your hands, which are now locked together, in a semicircle, first towards the opponent's waist and then up as far under his armpit as you can manage. Try to feed his hand into his armpit. Now hold his wrist down and lift up your head-hand arm to place pressure on the shoulder joint. Very little movement is needed if you have his hand far enough into his armpit.

The Americana is sometimes known as a reverse Kimura, as this is exactly what it is. The opponent's arm is bent and pointing upwards towards his

My hand is towards my waist, so Nate (top) goes for a Kimura. He holds my hand down, palm-down, with his "waist" hand (i.e. the one nearest the waist) while preparing to slide his "head" hand (the one nearest my head) under my arm.

Nate slides his "head" hand under my arm and pushes my arm up towards it with his "waist" hand. His "head" hand is effectively a trap, and he's pushing his other hand towards it.

Nate's "waist" hand reaches the trap and it snaps shut, locking his arms in a figure-4 position.

Nate applies the lock by lifting up my shoulder as if rolling it towards my feet. With my hand locked in place like that, the strain on the shoulder is enough to force a tap.

head, so you hold down his wrist with your head hand. Your head hand may be under his head or free; the technique can be applied either way. In this case his palm is up.

Your waist hand is placed on the mats, palm down, to make a ramp and the opponent's arm is pushed onto it. Slide your waist hand underneath and grasp your head hand wrist. Set up the lock by pulling the opponent's arm in close to his body and also towards his waist, then crank the shoulder to obtain the submission.

Americana can also be used from the mount. Grab the opponent's wrist and push it down beside his head, then reach under his head with your other hand and grip his wrist, trapping his arm. Now feed your free arm through between his forearm and upper arm and grip your wrist, locking your hands firmly. Roll the shoulder of the arm that's not under his head forward to crank the lock on.

This time my hand is up, towards my head, so Nate (top) applies an Americana or reverse Kimura. He pins my hand down, palm up, with his head hand.

Nate's waist hand goes under my arm and forms the trap. Nate pushes his head hand towards it.

The trap closes and the technique is locked in place.

Nate keeps my hand pinned and rolls my elbow upwards, placing strain on the shoulder and forcing a submission.

The same technique can be applied from an under-the-head hand position. Nate has pinned my hand close to my head.

He forces his waist hand under my arm and grips his wrist to secure his hands in position...

... and cranks the lock.

Using Submissions and Destructions

Submissions are primarily sporting tools. In a fight for survival you would not normally roll around looking for an arm bar then allow the opponent to tap out—if you release him then he may attack again. However, locks and chokes can be used to control an opponent, which may be appropriate. And of course, any joint locking technique can be used to destroy the joint. If you do need to break a limb to disable an opponent, do it immediately rather than putting a submission hold on and tightening it.

There are three reasons for this. Firstly, it is generally easier to break a joint this way, because you're using your weight when falling back for an arm bar. Secondly, you do not want to be tied up with an opponent in a situation where others might join the fight. Thirdly, it might be difficult to justify slowly breaking a joint when your opponent is helpless. It might look a bit more like slow torture than self-defense to others, and this could lead to legal complications. As noted earlier, reasonable force can be used in self-defense, and if breaking a limb really is necessary to stop an assailant then this would normally be seen as reasonable. If you have to do it, do it straight away and disentangle yourself.

In a sporting context, submissions are an excellent way to end a fight but you will rarely get the first one you attempt. It is usually necessary to "chain" techniques together or to use an attempt at one to distract the opponent

Here, Gary (bottom) has managed to push his opponent's arm across his throat, breaking his body structure and perhaps setting up a triangle choke.

As the opponent tries to get out of this suddenly dangerous situation, Gary gets the opportunity to turn him over and obtain a dominant position. He might or might not manage to apply the triangle choke, but Gary has improved his position in the fight.

Nate (top) attempts a one-handed bar choke, knowing that his chances of success are not great.

Sure enough, the opponent attempts to counter by pushing the choke off his throat.

Nate's arm is briefly across his own throat, but so is his opponent's. Both fighters are vulnerable...

... but Nate was expecting this, where his opponent was thinking defensively. Nate grabs the opponent's arm and hauls it right across his throat...

... then hooks his arm around the opponent's head as he drops his weight onto the choking arm...

... and squeezes to apply the choke.

Nate attempts to apply an Americana, but the opponent is successfully resisting.

Nate switches tactics, suddenly pulling his opponent's arm across his throat.

Nate secures the arm by dropping his weight onto it, feeding his hand under the opponent's head.

Nate brings his hands together to lock in the position, and squeezes.

from something else. You can, of course, deliver knee and elbow strikes and punches while looking for a submission, or use a submission attempt that has not worked to immobilize the opponent while you strike him.

By way of an example, you might take the mount and try for a one-handed bar choke, knowing that the opponent will defend against it. If he doesn't, you've won. The commonest defense is to push your arm off his throat by shoving your elbow in the direction your hand is pointing. But this brings his own arm across his face. If you're quick you can grab his arm and hold it there, pushing behind his elbow and then moving in close to prevent him bringing the arm back. You can now reach under his head and grab his wrist, and you've got a triangle choke that he probably can't escape.

Chokes and locks can also be used to move the opponent around or put him where you want him. For example, an arm bar can sometimes be obtained in a standing position, but it is difficult to prevent the opponent from escaping by changing position. However, the technique can still be used to advance your position. Imagine you evade a lead-hand punch by stepping outside it and pushing it away with your left hand. Hook your left hand over the opponent's arm (don't try to catch a wrist that's not pinned to the floor, use a scooping action instead) and pivot in so that your right forearm is pushing on the back of the opponent's triceps. Pull with your left hand and push with your right arm, stepping in so that your right hip is as close as possible to the opponent's armpit.

This position is used as an arrest and restraint technique and as a weapon disarm by military and law enforcement personnel. It is difficult to maintain however, the opponent will usually manage to wriggle or roll out of an armlock applied from this position. However, you can use the locked arm to force him down, landing face first with one arm out to the side. If this happens, get your weight behind his shoulder to keep him down and bring your right arm under his chin, setting up a rear naked choke.

It is well worth reiterating that a good position is necessary before trying for a submission. An opponent's ability to resist can be reduced by distractions such as strikes, or techniques can be "chained" so that an attempt to defend against one set him up to be locked into the next. Most importantly, do not waste energy on submissions that have no chance of success; put yourself where you can succeed and then make the attempt. A good submission fighter is a bit like a disease; the opponent might not be aware that he's in trouble at first, but he will gradually and inevitably be destroyed.

This position is a staple of law enforcement and security control & restraint techniques. It makes use of a locked straight arm (an arm bar by any other name) and broken body structure to put the subject where he can be controlled or secured.

CHAPTER 13

Putting It All Together

Training Safely and Effectively

Once a fight starts, whether it's in the ring or cage, or outside a nightclub at 2 a.m., you fight with what you have. What you have is determined to some extent by genetics—there's a limit to how strong or fast you can get, no matter how hard you try—and by what you've been doing in training. That part you do have a choice about.

Training can be general or aimed towards a particular goal, with a slightly different emphasis in each case. General training is all about building a better fighter; technique work, physical development, conditioning, and so forth are all wrapped around one another and are aimed at causing ongoing improvement in your fighting capabilities. The most obvious goal-specific training is fight preparation. It can also mean preparing for gradings (which can be much the same thing in some martial arts!) or working towards a specific training goal such as mastering a new set of submissions.

The key to any successful takedown is establishing a good, effective grip on the opponent. This can be a challenge, so it is worth including competitive "stand-up grappling," working for a grip and takedown against an opponent doing likewise, in your training repertoire.

The "gloves vs. grappler" drill is a variant on focused sparring or rolling. One
partner can only strike (decide on a level
of contact before you start). The grappler
must close in and get his opponent under
control or take him down; the striker can
make that as hard as he likes while delivering strikes whenever possible.

You can train specific skills by setting up
a situation and then trying out various
options from there, either as a drill or
competitively. The aim here is to get past
the partner's guard (any way that you
can) within a prearranged time. Attacker
and defender then swap positions and try
to get past quicker or hold out longer.

In all cases, training needs to be as safe as possible. That does not mean
" completely safe"—fight training cannot be both effective and completely
safe. However, risks must be managed; injuries can disrupt training in
the shorter term and can affect a fighter's long-term career. Thus training
should mostly be low-risk skills or conditioning work, with limited but
intense application work.

The more time spent in higher-risk activities (heavy sparring, full-intensity rolling and the like) the greater the chance of injury. However, these
activities are essential to good fight preparation, and not just for the physical benefits. The mind must also be conditioned so that the fighter can
learn to function intelligently rather than relying on panicky responses
when under pressure.

The single greatest asset to fighter training is a good partner or a team
who work together well. It has been wisely said that "you're only as good
as your training partner allows you to be." You have to be willing to accept
a certain amount of pain in order for your training partner to develop his
skills, but good training is a two-way street; it's your turn next.

There is nothing wrong with refusing to train with someone who takes
liberties or who makes you uncomfortable. Some martial artists and fighters
are very heavy-handed with their training partners, but unwilling to take
the same in return. You're better off without people like that for all kinds
of reasons. You have the right to choose who you allow to hurt you, and

Striking drills can be tailored to specific circumstances, such as "sparring" from a disadvantaged position such as under the mount. The fighter on the bottom must work for a reversal while defending himself against his opponent's gravity-assisted shots.

how much. After all, it's you that bears the consequences if your training partner cranks a lock after you tap out, or whatever.

Having established a good partnership and mutual trust, you can train very hard and push the limits in the knowledge that if something goes wrong it's a genuine accident. This is where it becomes possible to train with hard contact and full resistance, and thus to begin to reach your true potential.

Good training partners learn to put aside their knowledge of what's coming next and just do what they are supposed to do. For example, imagine you are training defenses against a double-leg takedown. A bad training partner knows you are about to sprawl and either counters you or comes in half-heartedly. A good partner just tries for a double-leg as if he was going for one for real—he is, in fact.

If you go down and the opponent doesn't, it is wise to immediately get your feet towards him. The attacker will naturally try to get quickly past your legs. This can make a useful warm-up drill; the attacker tries to get around into position to kick from the side, and the defender tries to keep his feet in the way.

A useful training exercise is to execute a technique or take a position, then stop and think about your options for a moment. Chances are you habitually do the same thing from any given situation, but a moment's thought can throw up other options. Try them out, find out which ones work well, and add extra options to your repertoire.

Effective training should take the fighter outside his comfort zone, but only in measured amounts. There is no point in destroying his confidence by making his favorite techniques fail all the time, but it is worth learning to deal with that awful moment when the never-fails knockout shot just bounces off.

Some training time needs to be devoted to adapting to changed or disadvantageous circumstances, overcoming disappointment and dealing with situations that go horribly wrong for no apparent reason. Something as simple as telling the fighter that he is to do three 1-minute bouts in quick succession and tacking an extra one on when he thinks he's finished will help build mental toughness and the ability to get his head back in the game despite the disappointment of thinking he's won then seeing the opponent come right back after taking that fight-ending shot.

Overall, effective training is a combination of developing skills then applying them under increasingly hostile circumstances. Resistance should be built up gradually, until the fighter is capable of dealing with whatever happens in a rational and determined manner. Too much, too soon is as counterproductive as poor training.

Winning The Fight

Winning a fight is a matter of overcoming your opponent's physical and mental resilience before he overcomes yours. It is possible to simply bull through and win on sheer toughness and strength, but the price tag in terms of punishment you will have to take can be high. Fighting smart is as important as fighting hard.

A Gameplan is an essential tool. You need to know what you intend to do before you enter the arena. Your gameplan can be quite general (e.g. "Keep my distance, wear him down with kicks before I look for a finish") and it needs to be somewhat flexible. But what you cannot afford to do is to allow the opponent to dictate the course of the fight. If he has a plan that plays to his strengths and you do not, he will force you to fight on his terms and you'll probably lose.

Sometimes your game plan turns out to be the perfect set of tactics. You go in, nullify the opponent's best skills and comprehensively defeat him. More often, things go wrong, and your gameplan must not become a strait-jacket. You may find that it is invalidated by your opponent's strengths. For example, if you want to seek a submission on the ground but it turns out that your opponent is a superior grappler, you will need to change your plan. Don't abandon your gameplan at the first setback, but do be willing to swap tactics around if what you're doing is getting you into trouble.

If your corner is on the ball, he will have observations and suggestions between rounds, or shouted out during the fight. However, you must be prepared to look at what the opponent is doing and make your own decisions. If it's obvious to you right now that he's a great striker then there is no point in waiting for your corner man or coach to tell you that; you need to nullify those skills before you eat too many shots.

If you do abandon a plan, then don't just go to autopilot. You need to make a conscious decision to do something else. "Stay back and kick isn't working" must be followed with a decision to move to some other plan, e.g. "Clinch up and soften him with knees, then look for a takedown and ground-and-pound."

Obviously, your gameplan is not the only thing you can do. It is more of a statement of intent or acknowledgment of your strengths to guide you when you need to make a snap decision about what to do. If you want a standup fight, this does not preclude taking the opponent down at some point. But by formulating a plan you give yourself a route to follow. When you're under severe pressure that can be like a lifeline. A fighter who doesn't know what to do is halfway beaten, but one who can see that he must fight his way out of his current bad situation and get back to his plan has a clear goal. That can make all the difference.

Using Mobility is a key skill that needs to be habitual. Tired fighters tend to be easy to hit because they stop moving around so much, and often end up standing square on, directly in front of the opponent. Similarly, it is common for fighters who are under pressure to forget about maneuvering and to just bang away at what's in front of them.

Mark (left) has decided to shoot in for a leg takedown, and Chris has correctly read his intentions.

Chris moves back and Mark's shoot has already completely failed. But he's heavily committed and can't stop.

Mark crashes to the ground. In the class a failure is embarrassing, but that's the place to make mistakes like this one. If you learn from it, then the experience is not wasted.

Mobility must become a habit, just like keeping your guard up. Keep moving, changing the distance between you and the opponent. You can create doubt about what you are planning to do just by opening or closing distance; once you stop doing this it becomes easy for the opponent to read you and deal with your attack—or launch one of his own.

Mobility can be a sort of passive defense that you may not be aware of much of the time. If your opponent wants to shoot in or launch a striking attack, he needs the distance to be right or he knows he will fail. You will not always know when he decides not to make the attack because the distance has just changed, but you will benefit from limiting his options all the same.

Occasionally you will see an attack start and be aborted, or fall short because you moved out at just the right time. This is proof that your footwork is working for you, but most of the time you need to take it on faith that you are benefiting from the habit of staying mobile. If you stay still the opponent will be able to set up his attacks at just the right distance, and you'll notice that when it happens!

Mobility also conceals your intentions. If the only time you step forward is when you're about to attack, then the opponent will soon realize this and your attacks will fail more often, or run into a well-timed counterattack. On the other hand, if your preparatory step looks just like all the other ones that were not followed by an attack, the opponent gets less warning and your chances are better.

Timing, Rhythm and Cadence all refer to the way you move and attack. Most fighters have predictable timing; a lead will be followed by a cross after a predictable (if short) period. Timing is partially dictated by physical factors (e.g. your reach or how long it takes to drop into a shoot after throwing a shot as a distraction) but also by rhythm. The vast majority of fighters drop into a rhythm when working the bag or pads, and the same timings come out in a fight.

Cadence is all about breaking or changing this rhythm. An opponent who has got used to the timing of your lead-cross-roundhouse kick combination (or anyone's; it's a common enough combination and the timing is usually similar) will adjust his defense to accommodate. If he deals with the strikes and goes to cover the kick, only to find that it's not there, he suffers an instant of mental dislocation while he absorbs this information and reacts. Breaking the rhythm might allow you to land the kick just after he has aborted his defense, thinking the kick is not coming. You could also use a different combination, but that's not cadence as such.

Cadence applies to movement as well as attacks and defenses. Your opponent will often match your speed, so if you do everything at full speed, he will react at the same speed. If you can slow down a little when there is little risk in doing so, then come in as fast as you can, his reaction speed will have been adjusted to what he expects from you, which can get you past a defense that would otherwise succeed.

Combinations and Sequences are slightly different things. A combination is essentially a single attack made up of components delivered in rapid succession, e.g. a lead-cross combination is basically one attack comprising two blows. Combinations are a staple of striking technique, but sometimes it is more appropriate to deliver a sequence of attacks instead.

At risk of splitting hairs, a sequence differs from a combination in that it is not a set-piece but instead is a series of separate attacks. There is a gap (often a very tiny one) between techniques in which the fighter can observe results and decide what to do next. This can be important for two

Nate (left) has decided to arm bar his opponent, but before he can do that he has to complete several in-between steps. If any of them fail, he won't get to the end of his planned sequence. First he launches a single-leg takedown...

... which works.

Nate must now get past his opponent's legs, which he accomplishes by throwing the nearest leg violently to the side. This causes the opponent to roll away from Nate as he moves forward.

Nate prevents his opponent from rolling back or perhaps using his legs to defend with by jamming his left knee against the opponent's hip. He has given himself a clear shot at the head, which the opponent will find hard to defend against from that position.

reasons. Firstly, many fighters rush through combinations to get to the big shot at the end. This should not be happening, but it is a common tendency. Secondly, if you are in the habit of delivering a certain combination you may end up throwing the second or third moves even though the first has invalidated it.

The opponent's only real option is to use his left arm to protect his head. That puts the arm where Nate can grab it…

… which he does. Nate can now step round into position for his arm bar, with one foot either side of the opponent's arm.

He then drops back and throws his leg over the opponent's head….

… and, since all the intermediate steps succeeded, Nate can now apply his arm bar and win the fight.

By way of an example, you might train lead-cross-lead hook-uppercut as a combination (and why not? It's a good one!) and be in the habit of unloading it. Then one time your cross causes the opponent to flinch backwards at a strange angle for some reason. Your lead hand hook will be halfway to the target before you've registered that it's going to miss.

A sequence of separate moves is a little slower than a typical combination, but that's not a problem; each one that lands buys you time for the next. What it does is to encourage you to get your money's worth out of each component, throwing it as if it was the only thing you were concerned about at that moment. And if the opponent ducks or flinches in a way that makes your next movement invalid, you have an instant to realize this and go for something else.

Transitioning refers to changing position, grip, level, or technique. It is a critical skill that is often overlooked. Everyone would like to be 100% successful with everything they are doing, but it's never going to happen. You need to be able to switch to doing something else if your opponent is successfully defending. Transitioning is also vital if you want to get the most from your various different bodies of technique.

You may have a great roundhouse kick and excellent clinch work, but how well can you tie them together? A good transition allows you to bang the kick in and use it to cover you as you close the distance and establish a solid clinch. Get it right and you can start delivering knees while the opponent is still staggered by the kick.

Transitioning is equally important on the ground and standing up. If you're failing to get a Kimura from side control, you can keep at it or look for something else. You might have better luck with an armbar from mount, but first you've got to get to the mount without the opponent stopping you. The same applies in standup; you might want to transition from striking to a clinch and takedown, or get out from a bad position in close.

Transitions need to be smooth, quick, and above all, sudden. An opponent who feels you prepare to move or shift your grip may be able to stop you. If he's a split second behind you then your action will beat his reaction every time. This is important because you are vulnerable while

It is necessary to move seamlessly between ranges and bodies of technique (long-range striking, clinch striking, take-downs, grappling etc), or you will give your opponent opportunities to counter-attack. I've thrown a straight right...

... which served mainly as a distraction to allow me to move in close for an elbow strike.

I then shoot my left arm around the opponent's head for a clinch...

... and bang in a knee strike.

I use the knee strike to set up a simple drag-and-rotate takedown...

... which puts me where I wanted to be in the first place.

moving from one thing to another so you must not give your opponent a chance to counter.

Transitions can be drilled as technique sequences. Obvious choices include a lead-cross followed by a shoot or clinch; positional changes on the ground, e.g. from side control to mount, or combination takedown attempts such as coming in for a body lock takedown which your partner prevents, so you change level and dive in for the double leg instead.

Final Notes

In this book we have presented a basic body of technique and the intangible factors that bind it all together to create a fighter. This is a starting point only; you will probably want to add more techniques as your skills develop. But more importantly, we can only show the way. There is no substitute for doing the work, and if you are going to fight then you will need to do a lot of work.

Anyone who comes out to fight is worthy of respect, and so is anyone willing to commit to the endless grind of training. Those few glorious minutes in front of a crowd are bought at the price of hours in the gym and on the mats. Win or lose, every fighter has paid a steep price just to be there. Those that win are often the ones who went a little bit further, dug a bit deeper, and put in the extra work to give them the edge.

You might think you've got so much talent that you won't need to work so hard. If you think that, best give up now, because you'll find out painfully that it's not true. You can't just come out and win by talent and guts alone. Not outside the movies, anyway.

Winning a fight is as much about preparation as what you do in the fight itself. Skills and physical attributes such as strength and fitness are guided by an understanding of tactics and driven by a will to win. These factors are developed in training, tested in sparring, and brought to the arena ready to meet the challenge.

Victory will usually go to the fighter who makes better use of his advantages than his opponent, though upsets do occur. Anyone can eat that one punch that takes them out of the fight. A supremely skilled and well-conditioned fighter can collapse in the face of a somewhat inept but incredibly determined opponent. But if you had to bet, you'd probably bet on the best-prepared fighter. So it makes sense to try to be that better-prepared fighter.

A fight is best considered as a game of odds, and good preparation stacks the odds in your favor. For example, if the opponent is less fit and conditioned than you, he is likely to fatigue first and become an easy target. If you fight smart enough, you can nullify the opponent's advantages and play to your own strengths to the point where the fight is almost one-sided.

The truth is that fights are won in training and lost in the cage or ring. That is to say, if you train properly then you will have all the tools you need to win. There are no guarantees of course, but there is no shame in coming second to a superb athlete who simply outfought you—or who stacked the deck more in his favor than you did through harder training.

You can lose by failing to use your tools intelligently or by simply giving up. That's not the same thing as being defeated by a superior opponent; the fault here would be yours rather than the credit being his. You don't want that to happen, so you must train mental toughness and in-fight adaptability as much as you build muscle and drill your techniques. Only by developing as a well-rounded fighter, able to fight smart and keep going when it gets tough, can you give yourself a fair chance at victory.

And if you are going to put yourself in harm's way, you really deserve that... don't you?

This is an arm bar, the other way up. It's not how Keith intended to win this one, but by keeping his head he has found an opportunity and made the most of it.